MAKING BREAKTHROUGH INNOVATION HAPPEN

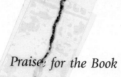

Praise for the Book

'In a knowledge society, we have to make innovations continuously. Innovation can start anywhere—from a fisherman's hamlet or a farmer's household or a classroom to a lab or an industry or an R&D centre.'

—A.P.J. Abdul Kalam

'This book on breakthrough innovations by Indian companies, NGOs and the bureaucracy distinguishes itself by its detailed focus on the thought processes which inspired and sustained the breakthroughs'.

—Ratan N. Tata

'A very inspiring book on orbit-shifting innovations taking place in India across corporate, social and public sectors. I highly recommend this book!'

—Jagdish N. Sheth, Professor of Marketing, Emory University, Atlanta, and Author, *Chindia Rising*

'This inspirational book uses the experiences of outstanding innovators to encourage others to move beyond their set orbits.'

— K.V. Kamath, Managing Director and CEO, ICICI Bank Limited

'Readers will be inspired by the real and practical stories of how passionate and persistent people can accomplish what others think is impossible.'

—Ram Charan, Business Advisor and Bestselling Author

'The book unravels to the reader the "essence" and "Indianness" of successful innovations that defied conventional wisdom—yet were very successful. A must-read for all those interested in fostering change …'

—Montek Singh Ahluwalia, Deputy Chairman, Planning Commission

'Innovation and entrepreneurship are two sides of the same coin, as is evident from these brilliantly compiled stories …'

—Ashok Ganguly, Chairman, First Source

'A must-read work of great inspiration.'

—R. Gopalakrishnan, Executive Director, Tata Sons

'The overwhelming feeling after reading the book is not only that "we can do it", but that "we can do it in our own Indian way". A must-read for all those involved in building an inclusive, innovative India.'

—R.A. Mashelkar, Chairman, Marico Innovation Foundation

'Provides insightful case studies from diverse contexts … highly relevant'.

—N.R. Narayana Murthy, Chairman and Chief Mentor, Infosys

MAKING BREAKTHROUGH INNOVATION HAPPEN

HOW ELEVEN INDIANS PULLED OFF THE IMPOSSIBLE

PORUS MUNSHI

Marico Innovation Foundation
Erehwon Innovation Consulting

COLLINS BUSINESS
An Imprint of HarperCollins *Publishers*

First published in India in 2009 by Collins Business
An imprint of HarperCollins *Publishers* India
a joint venture with
The India Today Group

Copyright © Erehwon Innovation Consulting 2009

ISBN: 978-81-7223-774-5

8 10 9

Porus Munshi asserts the moral right to be identified
as the author of this book.

HarperCollins *Publishers*
A-53, Sector 57, NOIDA, Uttar Pradesh – 201301, India
77-85 Fulham Palace Road, London W6 8JB, United Kingdom
Hazelton Lanes, 55 Avenue Road, Suite 2900, Toronto, Ontario M5R 3L2
and 1995 Markham Road, Scarborough, Ontario M1B 5M8, Canada
25 Ryde Road, Pymble, Sydney, NSW 2073, Australia
31 View Road, Glenfield, Auckland 10, New Zealand
10 East 53rd Street, New York NY 10022, USA

Typeset in 10.5/15 Giovanni Book
Jojy Philip New Delhi - 15

Printed and bound at
Thomson Press (India) Ltd.

CONTENTS

FOREWORD

THE INDIA ELEVEN

When you think of innovation, which companies come to mind? Apple, 3M, Google, Sony? Perhaps Dupont, Microsoft, Starbucks and Virgin? Can you think of an Indian company? Rarely does the name of an Indian company come up at first thought, or even as a second thought. When prodded, most people scratch their heads, pause, think, and then a name or two gets mentioned almost as an afterthought.

Why does this happen? Is it because there are no Indian innovations worth talking about, or is it because we don't know of them, or is it simply because we as a race are just too critical of ourselves and in too much awe of the developed world to believe in ourselves and in what we have accomplished.

Are we merely going to be the land of Jugaad—where quick-fix improvisations are used to tackle life's hassles? How can we take this intrinsic ability to improvise, and convert it into a national advantage? How do we move from small-time jugaad to high-value and high-impact innovation?

The last decade has seen the emergence of true innovation in

India. We have seen Indian companies being acknowledged as innovators in software services, pioneering the creation of entirely new industries like KPO (E Value Serve). From cloning, copying and improvising products, we are now beginning to create breakthrough products. Indian companies have clearly surfaced as pioneers in creating new models to capture the value at the bottom of the pyramid. Further, we have started to innovate for global markets too. Companies are now beginning to beat and not merely meet global benchmarks. It is possibly the onset of an innovative India where we are starting to challenge existing legacies; an innovative India where Indian entities of MNCs are becoming a springboard for innovation and aren't just clones of a distant parent; a changing India where government institutions are innovating to impact public services too.

This book is a culmination of a six-year joint discovery effort of Erehwon Innovation Consulting and the Marico Innovation Foundation. This endeavour aims at identifying genuine breakthrough innovations from within India and then uncovering cutting-edge insights into *what these innovators did differently to make the impossible happen*. The eleven innovations covered in this book provoke a change of reference points across industries and domains. The book will spark new insights into:

1. *Innovating legacy mindsets*: Established industries are usually populated with old and rigid mindsets. These legacy attitudes cut across all players in the industry, leading to a disease of sameness—everything, from products, packaging and promotions to advertising, looks the same.

Innovating in an industry steeped in legacy requires the courage to challenge and go beyond well-entrenched paradigms. This is very difficult in a hierarchical culture like ours. Take the hundred-plus-year-old newspaper industry. Legacy mindsets in an old and established industry like this are huge, like the belief that it takes years to establish a leadership position. However, *Dainik Bhaskar* became market leader on Day One of launch in every city in Rajasthan, Chandigarh, Haryana and Gujarat, by using a radical marketing strategy.

Legacies in industries are difficult to challenge and organization legacies can be as tough to overcome. Organization legacy comes from past successes and deep-rooted culture. Chola Vehicle Finance brings alive what it takes to break through a risk-averse culture and unleash new strategies for quantum growth.

2. *Innovating to take on giants*: In many organizations, there is awe and fear of and a deference towards giants, towards size. The belief is that if we provoke a giant he will come after us and we can't take him on. We are too small, too helpless, too resource-starved, and too weak to challenge.

The last decade has seen the emergence of challengers like CavinKare and Su-Kam (and Nirma earlier). They have demonstrated how entrepreneurs can create winning ideas even in markets dominated by giants. The founders of both CavinKare and Su-Kam are not in fear of MNCs; they display a positive irreverence. They believe that they can take on MNCs with 'new insight ideas'. They are new reference points for all entrepreneurs —because they break the myth that R&D and technology-led innovation can happen only in large organizations. They demonstrate how often an entrepreneurial organization can be better at innovating.

3. *Innovating for underserved markets*: There are millions of consumers who earn between two and five dollars a day. This forms a huge unserved market and many organizations want to be able to tap into it. However, most companies employ a largely

imperialistic mindset while trying to succeed in underserved markets. They believe that a 'no frills, knocked down' version of a successful product or strategy will be good enough for 'these poor people'. They fail to realize that this market does not want a poor man's Citibank; they want a Grameen Bank.

ITC-IBD, the company behind the revolutionary eChoupal idea, is a reference point of how a large organization can create an innovative business model that caters to the unique needs of farmers. An organization in Madurai has innovated and created an innovative business model that provides eye care to the economically handicapped. Aravind Eye Hospital evolved an eye surgery technique that increases a surgeon's productivity by a factor of ten. The business model ensures that millions of poor, visually impaired people can be operated for free or nearly free, and that the hospital still makes 40 per cent operating profit. It performs 200,000 cataract surgeries a year, making it the largest ophthalmology institution in the world. Further, students from Harvard and Johns Hopkins come here for exposure and training. If an eye hospital in one of the quietest corners of India can become such a global benchmark, what's stopping the rest of us?

MNCs: Innovating to Go beyond Cloning Global Success

This streak of innovation in India is not just visible in local entrepreneurial organizations, but also in the Indian entities of global MNCs.

Bosch India has been made the centre of competence for a particular single cylinder pump, called the PF pump, used in diesel engines. For more than a decade, this centre of competence worked only at tweaking products developed in Germany and this too after extensive permission seeking. A crisis moved them from looking up to Germany to taking action on their own.

Today, they have created a breakthrough product that's taking the global diesel world by storm.

Both Philips and Microsoft are now using India as a lab to create breakthroughs for the world, rather than merely replicating global successes in India. What this represents is a fundamental shift from the past where, for MNCs, Indian R&D was either handling legacy technology or was merely a support for cutting-edge R&D in the West.

Innovating to Create Breakthrough Products and Not Just Services

Product innovation and India don't seem to go together at present. Software yes, BPO yes, low-cost manpower yes, but product innovation no. New products come out of the US, Europe, Japan, Canada, South Korea and even Taiwan and Brazil. But not out of India.

The Nano and The Edge, both from Tata—Tata Motors and Titan—are reference points for breakthrough product innovation in India. These are examples where an Indian company created products that the world had decreed impossible.

Transforming 'Sick Institutions'

What is your reaction when you have to engage with the police or a city corporation? Is it one of dread or hope? Sadly, it is one of dread and hopelessness. But even as the sickness of these two institutions that affect us on a daily basis deepens, there are examples of two innovations that are a source of hope.

The source of this transformation was a paradigm-shifting idea called 'community policing'. This transformation took less than two years in Trichy and has sustained even after the initiator, J.K. Tripathy, was transferred. Tamil Nadu is now taking this concept to Chennai, Coimbatore and Madurai. In Surat, S.R. Rao transformed conditions with a series of structural and process innovations. From a plague-stricken city it rose to become the second cleanest city in India.

Bureaucrats often hide behind myths like insufficient delegation of power, outmoded rules and regulations, and political interference. Tripathy and Rao demonstrate that the real insufficiency is that of leadership and the inability to lead transformation.

IN CONCLUSION

This book is not academic in style or content; it is deeply insightful and strongly provocative. It aims at instilling a constructive restlessness. And it hopes to inspire many new innovations.

This book is for corporates, from India and around the world, who want new inspirations and insights into innovation. It is for entrepreneurs who want to impact the world and not merely run a successful business. It is for professionals who want to create history and not merely follow it. It is for students who want to go beyond cribbing about today and create a new tomorrow. And finally it is for bureaucrats and politicians who are tired of living in denial and want to take charge.

This book is all this because it has been brought to life by Porus Munshi, whose capacity to pull out invisible but powerful insights is unparalleled. And when combined with his flair for writing, the result is compelling!

RAJIV NARANG
Founder, Chairman and Managing Director,
Erehwon Innovation Consulting

A NOTE ON THE BOOK

Marico Innovation Foundation was created in March 2003 to fuel innovation across India. We had some of the most eminent and influential innovation leaders in the country as members of its governing council. I was privileged to be invited to chair the council.

We were all concerned about how we could make the 'I' in India stand for 'innovation' and not 'inhibition' or 'imitation'. How could the 'I' in industry, in an IIT, in every Indian, stand for innovation? How could we create, by design, vast numbers of innovators and innovation leaders? How could we, as Indians, believe that innovation-led quantum growth could happen not just in the West but in India too? Who were the Indians who could act as lighthouses of innovation and whom others could emulate?

It is this concern that led us to undertake deep research studies on innovation in India. Erehwon, through its painstaking efforts, brilliantly designed and managed Marico Innovation Foundation's Challenger Research Projects.

The learnings from these studies are as insightful as they are illuminating. And the leading, truly inspirational, examples are compiled in this book. Here, you will see how the 'impossible' can be made into the 'possible'.

The intent of the Foundation is to disseminate the findings across the length and breadth of the country in the form of this book so that people are inspired by the fact that India can not only innovate but that it can do so in a way that is typically 'Indian'.

I hope the current and future generations in India will not only benefit from these learnings, but that they will make innovation a way of life, so that a truly inclusive, innovative India, one that we can be proud of, will be created.

R.A. MASHELKAR
Chairman, Marico Innovation Foundation

ACKNOWLEDGEMENTS

I have always skipped this particular page whenever I have read a book. It's only now after writing a book that I realize how much one truly depends on the work and support of others. It's never ever a solitary effort, even if the name on the title page stands alone.

This book would not have been possible without an army of people. It owes its origin to a research project initiated by Erehwon Innovation Consulting and the Marico Innovation Foundation. Rajiv Narang, founder and chairman and managing director of Erehwon, and Harsh Mariwala, chairman and managing director of Marico, were the initiators of this project. And in true innovator fashion they have been consistent non-dilutors in the journey from conception to final launch. Harsh has been an extraordinary supporter of the entire journey.

The council members of Marico Innovation Foundation have played a key role in this work. Besides being consistent and passionate crusaders for the cause of innovation in India, Dr Ramesh Mashelkar and the council members helped identify many of the innovators in this book. Ranjan Kapur in addition has been deeply involved in the final stages of the positioning and dissemination strategies of this book.

The path-breaking initial research was spearheaded by Erehwon's Devika Devaiah, director and practice head, Innovation Discovery and Technology, and Bhupendra Sharma, co-founder and director. They were assisted by Venkatesh Rao and Raji Daniel, manager and executive, respectively, of Research Initiatives. The innovator differentiators—Setting an Orbit-shifting Challenge, Challenging the Establishment through a Breakthrough Insight, Enrolling to a Cause, and Combating Dilution—were conceived and developed by Rajiv, Devika and Bhupendra.

I came in later and began to do further research on and write out some of the biographies of the missions that Devika, Bhupendra and Rajiv had identified, short-listed and researched. The writing went through numerous revisions until Rajiv finally said, 'Why don't you write in a manner that will inspire people to actually sit up and take action rather than just read an "interesting" story?' That was an 'orbit-shifting challenge', and the book you now hold in your hands is a direct result of that. The mission biographies you will read about have been prototyped at Erehwon workshops and read by hundreds of participants, most of whom felt inspired and moved to action by the possibilities and learnings the mission biographies threw up. Thanks, Rajiv, for that orbit-shifting challenge, for your enthusiasm and for that detailed and constantly enabling feedback.

Once the mission biographies had been prototyped successfully, finding a publisher was initially a challenge because the way these were written went against the 'usual' structure and format of a book. We felt that allowing them to make this a 'usual' book would compromise and dilute the undertaking.

Then Gita Piramal pitched in and suggested we talk to Krishan Chopra, publisher at HarperCollins. Krishan loved the idea of an inspiring, and sometimes openly provocative, book on breakthrough innovations in India. A large part of the credit for this book goes to Krishan Chopra. His openness, helpful hints and ideas on the flow of the book were invaluable. Amit Agarwal, managing editor at HarperCollins, worked on the material with the eye of a true dilution-combater and kept nudging and pushing for greater clarity, connectivity in text and for plugging any gaps in information. Thanks for that detailed eye, Amit. Shantanu Ray Chaudhuri, chief copy editor at HarperCollins, played a key role with his attention to detail and his inputs that helped drive consistency in the book.

Passionate crusaders from Marico have been Milind Sarwate, chief, HR and Strategy, Pankaj Bhargava, former chief, HR, and Namita Vikas, principal consultant. I thank Pankaj for his support and ownership and Namita for relentlessly driving the last mile. Her focus, dedication and effort in making the book happen have been awesome.

At Erehwon, thanks go especially to Ranjan Malik, partner consultant and practice head, Innovation Missions, who has always been a very vocal and strong supporter of anything radical in the organization. He was a very early supporter of this format of writing. Thanks also to Prabha Parthasarathy and Sujit Sumitran, partner consultants and practice heads for Leadership for Innovation and Firestarters respectively, for prototyping the mission stories in their workshops. Priya Iyer, business manager at Erehwon, is, and always will be, a rock when it comes to enthusiastically supporting every new endeavour. She is a true challenger every day of the week. Discovery consultants Madhujith Venkatakrishna and Chhavi Goyal helped with the insight dialogues for Titan Edge, Bosch and Su-Kam. Chhavi also wrote the initial Titan Edge, Bosch and Su-Kam mission biographies that I later built on. Her contribution has been invaluable in growing these three mission stories. Gerald Jaideep, Innovation Initiator, came in at the last mile and helped anchor the book. Erehwon and Marico live and breathe the orbit-shifting principles you will see unfolding in the book.

The Titan Edge, Bosch India and Su-Kam cases were made possible through a joint research partnership between Altair Engineering Ltd, a global provider of innovation technology, the Marico Innovation Foundation and Erehwon. Pavan Kumar, managing director, Altair India, and Nelson Dias, president, Altair Asiapac, were key champions from Altair.

Any acknowledgement would be inadequate without mentioning the dozens of orbit shifters I've encountered during the course of writing this book, each of whom has been an inspiration. These innovators brought home to me strongly how much orbit shifting is a mindset and approach rather than a process. You will meet some of these innovators in this book.

And finally, but by no means the least, thanks to Shireena, my wife, who sat up with me all those late, long nights, painstakingly going through and helping me rework every sentence, every phrase. Her gentle, constructive feedback helped structure the mission biographies and the book was crafted as much by her as by me.

INTRODUCTION

One key question has for long fascinated us at Erehwon Innovation Consulting and the Marico Innovation Foundation: *What does it take to make orbit-shifting innovation happen?* To find an answer we began the Challenger Research Project. We met over 180 people in organizations across forty industries and sectors and identified challengers or orbit shifters based on the criteria of impact, uniqueness and leverage. Once identified, we conducted first-hand and in-depth research into individuals and organizations that have made orbit-shifting innovation happen.

The driving force behind both Erehwon and the Marico Innovation Foundation was to find a way to help India become a truly developed nation in its own right. If the 1980s and 1990s were the decades of Japan and quality, can the 2010s and 2020s be the decades of India and innovation? Can we use innovation as a springboard to tackle the challenges facing India today? And could Erehwon and Marico, by identifying just what it is that makes such innovation happen, play a role in creating this desired future? The research study was the first step in this direction.

(Altair Engineering came in later as partners for a research study on what enables and hinders product innovation in India. Three mission studies emerged from this research: Su-Kam, Titan Edge and Bosch India.)

We were clear that this wouldn't be the usual research that determines what innovators *do* differently and then seeks to develop a how-to list of things to do. How orbit shifters do something is certainly interesting and useful. But to us what was more critical was how they think! As Dr N. Natchiar of Aravind Eye Hospital, one of the orbit-shifting innovators in our research, says, 'We keep sharing our best practices, processes and methods with other organizations ... But none of them is able to replicate what we do because they focus on the processes and not on the underlying philosophies that drive our organization.' Really, the internal leads the external. As long as we focus on the external manifestations and not on the internal mindsets and beliefs that drive orbit-shifting innovation, we are going to be focusing on the wrong things and true replication won't happen. Therefore, we decided to focus on the mindsets and patterns of thought and action that drive orbit shifters.

Choosing the Orbit-shifting Missions

We chose companies and missions based not on scale alone but on the fact that each of them had shifted their industry's or sector's orbit in some way. These companies and missions had defied conventional wisdom and instead blazed their own paths.

We chose such missions not just from the corporate sector but also from the public service and social sectors, as we felt that if a mindset was truly effective, it should hold true across sectors. Also, it's limiting to learn from just one sector when amazing breakthroughs were happening in different sectors, with lessons for all.

From the corporate sector we chose Dainik Bhaskar, ITC-IBD, Shantha Biotech, Titan, Bosch, Chola Vehicle Finance, Su-Kam and CavinKare. From the public service sector, we chose the makeover of Surat city and the transformation of the police force at Trichy. From the social sector, we chose Aravind Eye Hospital.

Except for Shantha Biotech, none of the organizations in the corporate sector is from a sunrise industry. And yet each has made radical growth happen. Shantha Biotech is certainly in a sunrise industry, but it's also an industry it helped create in India, facing tremendous challenges along the way. For instance, its applications to the government of India for permission to develop a genetically engineered r-DNA vaccine kept getting lost for several months. Then they found that the powers that be in government didn't quite understand what *genetically engineered* meant. Since the application had the word *engineered* in it, it was sent off to the Public Works Department!

What We Found

There is a pattern to making orbit shifts happen. Orbit shifters begin with a create-history kind of impossible challenge that engages the heart rather than appeals to reason. Next, they seek out cutting-edge insights to find ways of reaching that challenge. The breakthrough strategy emerges either from these insights or from a complete reframing of the established order. Then they constantly enrol the numerous stakeholders, gatekeepers, team members, influencers and regulators who can make or mar the mission. And not just enrol them, but actually infect them so that they become champions of the mission. And finally they consistently combat entropy and the near-inevitable dilution that takes place whenever something 'impossible' is attempted. It takes a hawk eye and a consistent 'maximizing' mindset to ensure that dilution doesn't happen.

From a personal angle, what comes across strongly in almost all the orbit shifters is a strong sense of character as defined by Stephen Covey in *The Seven Habits of Highly Effective People*. In these profiles you clearly see a strong character ethic: for instance, the Surat municipal commissioner, S.R. Rao, who stands in line to get a phone connection for his brother and doesn't use his Indian Administrative Service (IAS) credentials. Rao went through incredible hardships, threats and even family turmoil in his bid to clean up Surat, and yet he stayed the course. He talks about the 'character' required to do the right thing during tough times.

Varaprasad Reddy of Shantha Biotech leaned over his desk one day, looked me in the eye and said, 'Sir (he calls everyone 'sir'), whatever you do, never, never, never pay a bribe. It is this more than anything else that is pulling our country down.' And it's not surprising that this man faced incredible bureaucratic opposition and went through tremendous hardship before his vaccine saw the light of day. But, as he says, he has never ever paid a bribe.

Character, as people like Rao and Reddy define it, lies in always battling and overcoming the obstacles that come in the way of doing the right thing.

The intent of this book is to learn from exceptions. Exceptions and successes teach us far more than failures do because the routes to failure are many. The routes to success are often limited. Also, it's far more inspiring to learn from successes. Successes and exceptions point to possibilities. As long as even one person has been able to demonstrate what it takes to make orbit-shifting innovation happen, it can be done.

The Format of This Book

We have always had examples and case studies of initiatives in books, but rarely biographies of breakthrough missions. In this book, we focus not just on mindsets and examples, but also share complete biographies of eleven orbit-shifting missions with a running commentary that gives readers a sense of the drama, challenges, dilemmas and frustrations that each of them has gone through.

The mission biographies have also been written in a particular manner with boxes that provide pauses and triggers for reflection. These are there to help you reflect on what the orbit shifter does differently and how what he did can be replicated in your organization. The intent is to trigger, provoke and if possible, inspire other such missions. I am quite sure that there are a number of potential orbit shifters out there who need just a slight nudge to tip them over into actually making something breakthrough happen. I am hoping this book will provide that nudge.

We haven't left this nudge completely to hope. In true orbit-shifting fashion, we have prototyped the style of writing to ensure the nudge does occur. Each of the mission biographies here has been prototyped for impact with participants in Erehwon mission workshops. And the results have been very heartening.

1

THE DYNAMICS OF
BREAKTHROUGH INNOVATION

You can have the greatest ideas in the world, but that won't make you innovative. Contrary to popular belief, the starting point of a breakthrough innovation isn't an idea but an orbit-shifting challenge.

Arla Foods, the Denmark-based dairy products company, wanted to kick-start breakthrough innovation in the organization. They didn't start by collecting ideas. Instead, Michael Stevns, their director of innovation, sought a challenge that would push Arla out of its current orbit. And he found one that was literally orbit-shifting. He decided they would be the first to put milk and milk products into space. It had never been done before. Milk had never before been part of an astronaut's diet in space though the benefits were awesome. That single orbit-shifting challenge pushed Arla's R&D and product development teams completely out of their usual product development trajectory and they emerged with truly innovative products that could be used back on earth as well—for example, imagine a yogurt that needs no refrigeration and has a shelf life of two years! They emerged with the kind of products that they would never have dreamed of if they had stayed on planet Earth.

Take the Dainik Bhaskar newspaper group. When the group decided to expand dramatically, they did not seek ideas from the founding family or from the organization. Instead, they began with an orbit-shifting challenge: be the leader from Day One in every city of launch. In almost all of their launches, they did just that and, in a short period of time, they became one of the largest newspaper groups in India in terms of circulation. The orbit-shifting challenge gave them ideas that completely redefined how newspapers are marketed, launched and sold.

Ideas are certainly important in an innovation journey, but they are not the starting point. An orbit-shifting innovation is more like an expedition to scale an extreme peak that has never been climbed before. Both involve getting a team together, enrolling team members, getting stakeholders who put up the money, putting a strategy in place, and creating routes that don't exist. Innovation involves finding ideas at every step of the way in truly hazardous terrain—when it comes to doing something orbit-shifting, an organization's terrain is no less hazardous than that of an extreme mountain. It's about keeping motivation and enrolment going in team members. It's about constantly going up when the mind wants to go down. It's about battling the hundreds of storms and challenges that invariably strike every extreme expedition. Finally, it's not just about reaching the summit. It's about developing the capability to reach other summits.

Each of the orbit shifters we have studied and worked with has had to follow similar stages. Having identified an orbit-shifting challenge, they then need to find the strategy to reach there. Impossible challenges need out-of-the-box strategies. These strategies emerge from questioning and challenging the established way of doing something as much as from high-quality insights. And that's only the beginning of the journey. The far more challenging part comes next when the orbit shifter has to enrol the numerous stakeholders, gatekeepers, team members and just about anyone else who can help or hinder the mission. It's not an easy job. Each stage requires a specific mindset and approach.

Take enrolling. If the mission champion is not able to excite others and infect them with the larger mission and purpose or cause, the effort will never really shift orbits. Think of Homi Bhabha, the father of India's nuclear age. He had a scale and depth of thinking that was breathtaking. People in the nuclear establishment still speak of him with awe four decades after his death in 1966. And the direction he set for India's nuclear journey all those years ago is still being followed. With an aspiration of that magnitude, he had to enrol people to his cause, and he did it! Starting with the Tatas, whom he influenced into setting up India's first nuclear research institute, the Tata Institute of Fundamental Research—and this was even before India got her independence! Obviously, he also had to enrol and influence British regulators to allow him to set up the institute. He enrolled Jawarharlal Nehru, whom he met on a ship voyage before India became independent, and as prime minister of an independent India, Nehru was an ardent supporter without whom the project would never have taken off. Bhabha influenced the rich Parsis around Bombay to gift or sell their land to him cheap to enable him to set up the Indian Atomic Research Centre—renamed the Bhabha Atomic Research Centre after his death. And he constantly battled the dilutions and gravities resulting from the lack of self-belief that was a legacy of India's colonial past. He put together an amazing team of people, who have sustained his vision and dream. What does it take to infect so many different people like this?

In the next sections and chapters we shall look at some of these mindsets.

Section 1 deals with an orbit-shifting challenge as seen through the lens of two remarkable orbit shifters: Dainik Bhaskar and Aravind Eye Hospital.

Section 2 deals with developing a breakthrough strategy by challenging the established way of doing things and from insight mining. We shall look at this through CavinKare, ITC-IBD and Bosch India.

Section 3 deals with the challenges of enrolment and how three organizations—Trichy Police, Chola Vehicle Finance, and Titan Edge—enrolled their team members to go beyond business as usual.

Section 4 deals with combating dilution and we look at this through the lens of Shantha Biotech, the Surat transformation and Su-Kam.

The biographies of the missions are complete in themselves. And as you will see, they contain within them all the orbit-shifting challenges. The intent of placing them into sections is that some initiatives highlight more powerfully the challenges in specific areas. For instance, the Surat transformation highlights what it takes to constantly combat the storms that arise when anything orbit shifting is attempted.

Rather than being a step-by-step rule book, we use mission biographies to help you along if you should ever decide to take on an orbit-shifting mission. The stages you will go through will be similar to those described here. The sections will help you dip into what it takes to enable each stage. For instance, if you seek an orbit-shifting challenge, the mission biographies in Section 1 will help you. If you seek to create a breakthrough strategy, the missions in Section 2 will help you, and so on.

As you read the mission biographies, reflect on what stands

out for you. This will often mean that you have encountered something you are not doing but should be doing. Make a quick plan to immediately execute this.

Don't go industry-specific and look for insights based on the industry you belong to. Instead, look for the challenges faced and how they were overcome. For instance, Titan Edge gives insights into what it takes to make product innovation happen and the kind of mindsets one needs to grapple with. It doesn't matter what industry you belong to. The missions have been chosen from an innovation perspective and their learnings cut across industries and sectors.

SECTION I

SETTING AN ORBIT-SHIFTING
CHALLENGE

The first stage in breakthrough innovation is often the call to adventure. It's the dragon-slaying challenge that the orbit shifter takes on. And it is perhaps this more than anything else that enables ordinary people to do extraordinary things.

Eliminate needless blindness across the world! Eliminate Hepatitis B from India! Be the leader from the day of launch! Transform the police in six months! Transform Surat! What's common in all these is that each is a dragon that people have taken on and slain. Each is an orbit-shifting challenge taken up by ordinary people who have gone on to do extraordinary things.

The mindset really is one of taking on challenges that everyone else considers 'impossible'. S.R. Rao, the bureaucrat who cleaned up Surat after it had been hit by plague, took on a challenge that was considered 'impossible' and that no one else wanted since it was a potentially career-limiting move. But he took up the challenge and did it in twenty months flat. Today, thirteen years later, he is still a rock star for the Suratis.

The key operating or guiding principle here whenever faced with a challenge is, as my colleague Ranjan Malik says, 'Max It!' 'Maxing it' really means going for the maximum whether it is currently possible or not. It is going for the maximum good, going for the impossible, the maximum size, the theoretical best, the *complete* elimination of problems. Thus, Varaprasad Reddy went for the maximum: eliminate Hepatitis B in India. Dr G. Venkataswamy of Aravind Eye Hospital went for the maximum: eliminate needless blindness across the world. At

Titan, they went for maximum when Xerxes Desai gave the call to create the slimmest water-resistant watch in the world.

Unfortunately, 'Max It' as an operating principle is initially often hugely difficult to follow because it directly clashes with our usual way of doing things as developed over a lifetime. Almost all operating principles in society today are centred around preserving the status quo, not 'maxing it'. Think of proverbs such as 'don't rock the boat', 'let sleeping dogs lie', 'if it ain't broke, don't fix it'.

Also, look at the way we use the phrase 'let's be practical' or 'let's be realistic'. Being 'practical' or 'realistic' almost always means being pessimistic. Can't 'practical' and 'realistic' also be optimistic?

When faced with a challenge, what operating principle do you choose to follow? Do you choose to 'not rock the boat', be 'practical', in the pessimistic sense? Or do you choose to 'Max It!'? When S.R. Rao decided to clean up Surat, he didn't follow the principle of 'don't rock the boat'. If he had done that, Surat would still be filthy. The reason it's the second cleanest city in the country is because he chose to 'Max It!' Take the example of a packaging expert at an Indian pharmaceutical major. His boss told him that he expected an Asia Star packaging award. When we met him and asked him what he was aiming at, he said he was aiming for a couple of World Star awards. We said that his boss expected an Asia Star. He replied that that was his boss's expectation. For him only a World Star would do—and he achieved it. That's Maxing It!

It's a mindset of constantly stretching the boundaries of the possible. And the payoffs are often huge. An orbit-shifting challenge does more than merely set a reference point. It *transforms* teams and people. A challenge is the catalyst that creates new capabilities.

Many organizations and teams don't even attempt anything radical, leave alone orbit shifting. The first excuse is, 'We don't have the capability'. But really, it's the challenge that leads to capability. Not the other way around. When John F. Kennedy gave the call to put man on the moon, the Americans didn't have the capability. When Varaprasad Reddy gave the call to eliminate Hepatitis B from India, India didn't have the capability. When Xerxes Desai gave the call to manufacture the slimmest water-resistant watch in the world, his engineers told him they didn't have the capability. If the Swiss couldn't do it, how could they? But Desai and his team persisted. And lo and behold, the engineers found they had the capability, after all. When our assumptions about what we can do are based on what we have so far done, we limit ourselves.

How does one choose a challenge? Perhaps mountaineer Todd Skinner provides a hint: 'If you're not afraid, you have probably chosen too easy a mountain. To be worth the expedition, it had better be intimidating ... A mountain well within your ability is not only a misspending of resources, it is a loss of opportunity across a lifetime of potential achievement.'

In the biographies of the two orbit-shifting missions that follow, you will see how both *Dainik Bhaskar* and Aravind Eye Hospital took on intimidating mountains. They took on challenges that everyone considered impossible. And with the principle of 'Maxing It' continuously operating, both have transformed their respective industries.

2

DAINIK BHASKAR

NO. 1 FROM DAY ONE

In 1996, the forty-year-old Bhopal-based newspaper group Dainik Bhaskar had a circulation of 350,000 copies per day in Madhya Pradesh. By 2004, this had grown by more than 1000 per cent to 3.5 million (2.3 million in Hindi and 1.2 million in Gujarati across six states in India: Madhya Pradesh, Chhattisgarh, Rajasthan, Haryana, Chandigarh and Gujarat), making it one of the top twenty-five dailies in the world. In a little over ten years, Bhaskar has achieved circulation figures that others in the global newspaper business have taken nearly a century to achieve. Today Bhaskar has a collective circulation of approximately 4.4 million across its titles—*Dainik Bhaskar, Divya Bhaskar, Saurashtra Samachar, Prabhat Kiran, Business Bhaskar, DB Star* and *DNA*.

Bhaskar's rapid growth has occurred in an unlikely setting. All the large, powerful media groups in India are based in the English language. Although Hindi is the most widely spoken language in India, the vernacular press is highly segmented with small, regional papers holding sway. No local language newspaper has been able to cut across states the way English newspapers have.

Further, the newspaper business was, and still is, a game of slow growth over generations of readers. People don't easily change newspaper-reading habits and if they do, it takes several years of persistent wooing to get them to shift.

But consider this: In Jaipur, its first city of launch outside Madhya Pradesh, *Dainik Bhaskar* entered the market as number one with 172,000 copies on 19 December 1996. In its next new market, Chandigarh, it was again number one with 69,000 copies when it launched in May 2000. In its third launch—the state of Haryana—it entered as number one with 271,000 copies in June 2000. And in its fourth launch, in Ahmedabad on 23 June 2003, it entered as number one with 452,000 copies—a world record. It expanded into Gujarat in a matter of fifteen months, entering the two other major cities of Gujarat—Surat and Baroda. It currently has nine editions in Gujarat and is the largest circulated Gujarati daily with 11.5 lakh copies according to the Bureau of Circulation. It continued this in Punjab in 2006, launching simultaneously from Amritsar and Jallandhar with 178,000 copies. These are results that make one sit up and say 'Wow'!

The usual question is: How did the Bhaskar group increase circulation by a factor of ten in such a short time in such a hostile environment? The larger questions are: What did these guys do differently from the others in the newspaper industry? What is replicable in what they did and what can organizations in other industries learn from them?

To understand the nature of Bhaskar's achievement, you have to understand industry dynamics: Any industry is made up of a leader and followers. The leader is there by virtue of some outstanding strategy or because it began the industry. The followers try to emulate the leader but since the latter has enormous advantages of efficiencies and market share, the former never quite catch up, though they keep him on his toes. This pattern persists across industries and this state of affairs continues for years.

But one day, a 'Radical Innovator' arrives who thinks differently. Who thinks big and thinks hungry and finds a brand-new way of doing things and ruthlessly implements his vision. When that happens, the comfortable industry equations change and become topsy-turvy, and the entire industry undergoes a rapid restructuring. The Bhaskar group is one such radical innovator.

You may have heard about Bhaskar's achievements before and may also have learnt how they did it. You may even have thought that what the Bhaskar group did was interesting, but not quite 'relevant' to your industry. After all you are in oil or FMCG or garments or whatever. And what those guys did cannot happen to your industry. If you believe that, you are in trouble. Radical innovators like Bhaskar are becoming the norm rather than the exception. And if you are not one, you can become irrelevant very, very fast.

We are going to delineate the Bhaskar group's approach step by step to highlight what radical innovators do. We urge you to look beyond the actual mechanics of each step and into the essence of what was done. Reflect well: like you there are other people reading this. And one of them could be the next radical innovator in your industry!

The Orbit-shifting Challenge

From 1992 to 1995, the Dainik Bhaskar newspaper was the undisputed leader in Madhya Pradesh, displacing, they say, the newspaper *Nai Duniya*. Having become number 1 with some distance between them and their competition, members of the Agarwal family that controls the group—Rameshchandra,

Sudhir, Girish and Pawan—were now restless and were seeking the next challenge.

They spoke about entering new markets in new states, as most directors of organizations would do; and they even began exploring potential markets. They identified Jaipur, Rajasthan, as the market with the highest potential and began to discuss the mechanics of entering it. One day, they were discussing their hopes and aspirations for the future and the mood was quite upbeat ... nothing different so far from what a thousand other managers and directors do every day.

How do you plan your organization's future? In our experience, most organizations work strategy forward. They think up an outstanding strategy and, based on this, work out future projections of milestones and goals. But radical innovators like Bhaskar do the reverse. They first have a dream; an impossible aspiration and then work back from there, devising a strategy that can deliver on that dream.

But then the chairman, Rameshchandra Agarwal, remarked: 'It sounds as if your aspiration is to reach the heavens.' The sons said 'yes'. 'Do you know what you have to do to reach heaven?' Pause ... 'Die?' 'Yes. Are you willing to die for this aspiration? Think carefully. Because if you are not, we are better off here in MP where we have reached a comfort zone. If we want to grow and expand, we will need to become extremely uncomfortable. We will be the target of every newspaper group that is threatened by our aspiration. If we want to go ahead, we go ahead completely and hold nothing back. Are we prepared to disrupt our personal lives, our families, and go there into the market and battle like we have never battled before? It may take years. If you are willing to do that, we go ahead. Otherwise we don't.' The sons said they were ready and committed to doing whatever was necessary to make it happen.

So they decided to go ahead with Jaipur and Rajasthan. And since they were going to go all out, they decided that they would aim at being number 2 on the day of launch. It didn't make sense to them to aim any lower. After all, if you are going all out why aim at a piddling target? They would go in as a clear number 2.

It wasn't just something that was 'nice to aim for'. It was a clear intent: be number 2 on the day of launch. We've rarely seen companies bold enough to enter a new market with a clear, pre-declared intent of being number 1 or 2 at launch. For instance, when your company launches products and services in a new market, does it enter with an aspiration to become number 1 or 2 on the day of launch, or does it just aim to get an initial toehold and then slowly expand? How would your entry strategy be different if you entered with the clear intent to be number 2 from Day One? *And by the way, are you willing to 'die' to achieve your dream?* 'Die' is also a metaphor; what, in your current ways of thinking and working, has to 'die' in order to give birth to something remarkable?

When the Agarwals articulated their aspiration, they had no idea how to achieve it. They had no strategy or plan in place. All they had was their commitment that if they were to expand, they would go all out and think big.

For Bhaskar, it certainly wasn't an easy goal. Newspapers take decades to reach any sort of leadership position. And incumbent newspapers often enjoy a brand loyalty that other industries would kill for. Newspapers are perceived to be a morning habit and part of a person's morning ritual as much as tea or coffee. An added difficulty is that newspapers lose money in operations.

The more newspapers you sell, the more you lose money until advertising revenue catches up. But this often takes a long time. So the usual strategy is to grow a bit, wait for ads to come in, grow a bit more, and so on. A hugely painful process. But that's the way it's always been.

MEETING THE CHALLENGE HEAD-ON

When Bhaskar began with the aspiration of entering Jaipur as number 2 with a print run of 50,000 copies on Day One, it began the process of demolishing all the industry entry and growth barriers. Every industry paradigm would necessarily have to be rethought.

———

Every industry has its entry barriers and its growth barriers. And everybody in the industry operates within them. The entry barriers keep newcomers out and the growth barriers maintain the status quo. If you are number 1 or 2 that's a very comfortable situation. But sooner or later along comes a wild-eyed orbit shifter who refuses to play by the rules. *And suddenly all the barriers that you thought had foundations in concrete tumble like a house of cards.*

———

Therefore the group decided to go in for a truly in-depth understanding of the readership patterns in the city. Unlike a conventional survey that takes a random sample size and tries to extrapolate information into a broad need or trend, the Bhaskar group decided to meet a whopping 200,000 potential newspaper-buying households in Jaipur!

The intent behind the massive consumer contact programme was to personalize the newspaper. As Girish Agarwal, director of marketing and member of the core team, says, buying newspapers is a personal habit and little influencing takes place. We are very independent in buying a newspaper. Therefore it makes sense to talk to the customer as an independent entity ... But then buying soap and mobile phones and underwear are also personal habits. And how many consumers do the manufacturers of those products meet? I don't know about you, but no one has met me.

> When was the last time you actually listened to 200,000 of your consumers in one city? No organization that I know of has done this. Most surveys are puny affairs using 'representative samples' and 'statistical variances' conducted by market research companies, at the end of which nobody knows who's been met and who hasn't. But reports are churned out and the 'will of the consumer' is presented to senior management with bugles blowing and flags fluttering.

As the Bhaskar bigwigs began to immerse themselves in the mechanics of the survey, given its scale, it quickly became an integral part of their strategy. They decided not only to find out more about the customer and his needs but also to make it an *experience enhancing* contact with the consumer so that everyone 'surveyed' felt good at the end of the meeting with the Bhaskar surveyor.

We love that term—Experience Enhancing! So different from 'customer feedback' or 'satisfaction survey' or (yawn) 'client servicing'. *How does your organization Enhance the Experiences of your customers?* Actually, think about the 'Customer Service Department' that most organizations come up with. The term itself throws up images of someone being taken somewhere to be 'serviced' much like a car or a two-wheeler. How would the department function if its mandate was 'Experience Enhancing'?

Something so important could not be outsourced to any market research company. It had to be finely controlled and therefore done in-house. The survey was becoming the cornerstone of their strategy. They set up a team of 700 surveyors from scratch.

During the survey, an idea emerged: they would finish the survey and go back with the results to the households already met. From there, the next idea was: 'If we go back, can we ask them to sign up for an advance subscription?' This was a radical question. They were thinking of asking customers to pay upfront for a newspaper they hadn't seen. Rather than dismiss this as too radical, the team began working back from here.

They did their thinking in detail. Working back from the intent, they asked, 'If we do ask the customers to pay upfront, what comfort zone do we need to create within the consumer?' This threw up two follow-up questions: 'What are the major consumer concerns and forces of gravity in doing this?' And, 'How can they be overcome?'

The team realized that there were two major fears that customers had: the fear of being taken by surprise and getting something he/she didn't want, and the fear of losing money in a bad deal.

To overcome the first fear, the team hit upon the idea of *evolving the product with the customer*. So they went to each customer and asked him/her questions like: 'What are you not getting in your current newspaper that you would like to get more of?' and 'What would you like your newspaper to do for you?' Then, based on the feedback, *the survey team went back to all 200,000 households* to show them what they had created based on their feedback.

The entire survey team of 700 surveyors was highly trained in engaging with the consumer. Experts in the field taught them

Most surveys we know are superficial, insipid affairs with no genuine intent to engage with the customer. Both the surveyor and the customer are intent on just getting it over with. You can see it in their body language and you can see it in the apologetic way the surveyor approaches the consumer. Imagine actually meeting your usually faceless customer face-to-face and then allowing the meeting to go downhill ... What a huge opportunity loss.

body language, grooming, posture, approach methods, social norms and rules, and how to engage and converse with consumers.

This triple whammy of engaging with the consumer, involving him in creating the product and making multiple visits to him sharply reduced his fear of being taken by surprise. It got the customer thinking: 'I know these guys, they're pretty friendly. Also I've played an important role in creating the product and for once I know just what I'm getting.'

This set the stage for asking for the advance subscription of six months/one year. To overcome the consumer fear of losing money in a bad deal, the surveyor signed and gave the consumer a 'guarantee bond' that promised the consumer a subscription price of Rs 1.50 as against the newsstand price of Rs 2 and an immediate refund if he wasn't satisfied with the product. The bond also guaranteed that no matter what the fluctuations in newsstand price, the advance subscriber would get the newspaper at Rs 1.50. *The consumer now had no reason not to subscribe ... and subscribe he did.*

Dainik Bhaskar launched in Jaipur with 172,347 copies. Not as number 2, but as leader from Day One. The erstwhile leader, *Rajasthan Patrika*, which had assiduously built up its leadership position over thirty years and which had a circulation of 100,000 copies, was overthrown overnight! By a raw upstart.

As Girish Agarwal says, 'Always challenge conventional wisdom—the Pandavas did, and won the Mahabharat.

Conventional wisdom dictated that armies won wars and that they should have taken Krishna's army when it was offered. Instead, they refused the army and asked for Krishna alone—and that too as a non-combatant.'

Dainik's success at Jaipur is remarkable in itself and many organizations would have rested on their laurels, wallowing in self-congratulations. But the Dainik team went full steam ahead and, in keeping with their commitment to their chairman, continued with launch after launch. They did a Jaipur to Chandigarh, Haryana, Ahmedabad and Gujarat. Number 1 on the day of launch each time!

In Chandigarh, Dainik took on a city where English newspapers outsell Hindi ones by a factor of six! Selling Hindi newspapers in Chandigarh was considered impossible. But where others saw problems, this amazing team saw opportunities. So they hit the streets again in January 2000, this time in Chandigarh, and contacted 220,000 households. And as they did so, they found insights that nobody else in the newspaper business had, *because no one had met the common man*!

They found that *every* household in Chandigarh was comfortable with Hindi and in many cases more comfortable with Hindi than with English. And that they bought English newspapers not because they preferred the language, but because the quality was better.

For thirty years, more English newspapers sold in Chandigarh as compared to Hindi ones and everyone assumed that's the way the market was. In reality it was the *quality*, stupid. It was about *design* and content. It was about giving the consumer a newspaper he feels good holding.

Once Dainik realized that design mattered, they not only made design the king, they went a step further and incorporated the local Chandigarh dialect in the design. They mixed both Hindi and English in the newspaper, making it a true Chandigarhi newspaper.

This was awesome! At a single stroke they had created uncontested market space. You had English newspapers competing with each other and Hindi newspapers competing with one another. But you didn't have a Hinglish newspaper. It stood alone.

The result was that Bhaskar was the leader on Day One in Chandigarh. The erstwhile leader, the English-language *Tribune* (50,000 copies), was replaced by the Hinglish *Dainik* (69,000 copies at launch). Today *Dainik* is at 100,000-plus copies.

Another impact was that while the total readership of Chandigarh was 54 per cent of the population before Dainik, today it's 61.4 per cent. Dainik expanded the market.

> We tend to think in terms of identities. We *are* an English newspaper company or a Hindi newspaper company or a mobile or a watch manufacturing company. These identities trap us in worlds of our own making. A Hindi newspaper doesn't 'do' English. A mobile phone doesn't 'do' cameras or music or TV, a watch company doesn't 'do' jewellery ... until someone comes along who does, and you get done in.

That's what radical innovators like Dainik do. They expand the market. Incremental innovators focus on trying to grab market share from the competition and fight within the existing market space. But radical innovators go a step further. They create a brand-new space for themselves and bring in buyers from two streams: existing and brand new. What's your company doing? Battling harder and harder for customers who are getting fussier and finickier? Ever thought of looking outside your existing customer base? And if you've thought about it, what have you done about it?

After Dainik had stormed through Jaipur, Chandigarh and later Haryana, it zeroed in on Ahmedabad and decided to launch in Gujarati! What was a Hindi newspaper doing thinking of Gujarati?

The Gujarati-language newspapers in Ahmedabad thought they were safe and isolated from raging maniacs like the Dainik Bhaskar group (thank goodness they are a 'Hindi group'). You see the identity barrier kicking in again? And sure enough, they got Bhaskared! Dainik Bhaskar launched in Ahmedabad as *Divya Bhaskar* with 452,000 copies—a world record. And as leader from Day One. Naturally.

As we said at the beginning of this chapter, you may think that your situation is different and that your company or industry would react differently and not get Dainik Bhaskared by a radical innovator. You would be dead wrong.

In Ahmedabad, the competition was not caught napping. They didn't underestimate Dainik's capability once it became clear that they were going to enter the market. The leading Gujarati newspapers came together and held discussions with their Dainik Bhaskared counterparts in Rajasthan, Chandigarh and Haryana to understand how Dainik Bhaskar operated in order to pre-empt them. For instance, they came up with colour pages once they realized that Dainik Bhaskar had done this in both Rajasthan and Chandigarh. They even responded with price reductions and several high-value consumer offers. But it was too little too late.

> If there's one thing the Dainik story tells us, it's that the writing's on the wall. Do you see the writing on the wall? It reads: 'Arriving soon in your industry—Radical Innovators. Starring hungry, radical, orbit-shifting non-entities nowhere on your current radar.' Do you see it? The newspapers in Ahmedabad didn't.

They seemed to be just responding to Dainik Bhaskar's

initiatives. And if I were a regular buyer of these papers, that would make me mad. All these years I had been taken for granted and expected to lap up whatever was dished out because I had no choice. And when someone comes along who has not only visited me at home and asked me what I wanted but also co-evolved my newspaper with me, my existing newspapers have suddenly woken up and started giving me colour pages and freebies. Do I feel loyalty towards them? No way! I would march with my chequebook. And apparently that's just what many readers did. *Divya Bhaskar*, the Gujarati version of Dainik Bhaskar, launched with 452,000 copies and their collective Gujarat circulation is now 11.5 lakh. *Divya Bhaskar* both expanded the market as well as took the competitors' buyers away from them.

> Are you taking your customers for granted? Are you only giving them what you can get away with and what the industry norms prescribe? Or are you giving them what no one else can? If a hungry radical innovator were to come in today, what would he give your customers that's different from what you are giving? Different enough to cause a large-scale migration? Having reflected, what are you going to do about it?

THE MECHANICS OF THE DAINIK BHASKAR SURVEY

The Dainik survey is a remarkable undertaking. They build their own team of part-timers from scratch. For instance, at Ahmedabad, where they surveyed (and enhanced the customer experiences of) a titanic 12,00,000 households, they used 1050 surveyors, 64 supervisors, 16 zonal managers, and 4 divisional managers to run the show. It is possibly the single biggest direct consumer contact programme in history. And they met each household twice!

The people for the survey were gathered largely through posters at colleges and by word-of-mouth as the print advertisement channel was not available to Dainik Bhaskar and TV ad spots were too expensive. College campuses were targeted as well as graduates and first-time job seekers. The benefits promised were exposure to a truly unique real-time work experience, fun and, where possible, induction into the organization. For example, the Sikar unit head in Rajasthan was recruited from the survey. He was a surveyor in Jaipur. Nearly 40–50 per cent of surveyors were absorbed in *Dainik Bhaskar* or *Divya Bhaskar* based on merit. The rest were given a certificate of appreciation that stated their contribution in this massive effort.

The surveyors also knew that they were part of something unique—a mammoth experience that would look good on their resumes.

Intense training was conducted on their grooming, present-ability, etiquette, body language, social skills and methods of engagement. The training ensured a standardized contact method as well as standardized appearance and behaviour of the surveyors. Tracking teams were formed to ensure that the highest levels of engagement and social norms were adhered to. The surveyors did so well that when they went back for the second round, they were greeted like long-lost friends and welcomed back and often offered refreshments. Now that's what we call customer engagement and experience enhancing.

The survey team had a time frame of forty days in which to reach out to eight lakh households in Ahmedabad (plus four lakh in the adjoining districts). This gave the team a daily target of 20,000 households, with each surveyor expected to make a minimum of twenty productive calls. The primary respondent was identified as the chief wage-earner of the family.

Imagine if you will, a typical morning in Ahmedabad that begins before dawn with batches of around 200–300 surveyors in blue, cream and yellow congregating in the parks and gardens of the city. Their morning begins with a prayer and hymn from the film *Ankush*: *'Itni shakti hamay dena daata, mann ka vishwas kamzor ho na'*. With over 200 people in straight lines, singing in unison, it's a sight that gives one goose bumps.

This exercise makes the group feel that they are going on a mission to achieve something spectacular. Then, after a short briefing, they hit the road for their 20,000 productive calls for the day. They knock on doors and are supported by supervisors who closely monitor success, failure and behaviour aberrations and coach on the spot those surveyors who need help, or send them with others more successful to observe how they do it.

After the surveyors knock on the doors and get feedback, they give the residents a 'thank you' gift of a handbook on Ahmedabad and a calendar-panchang.

The day ends with an evening sit-down review where successes are highlighted, songs sung, and a general review and sharing of the high and low points of the day takes place, as well as a sharing of observations by the supervisors and managers. The data collected is given to the computer operators for keying in. Throughout, the focus is on fun and enjoyment along with learning and results.

At frequent intervals throughout the survey period, there are parties and functions with celebrities invited for the surveyors to interact with, as well as reward programmes for individuals and teams performing well. Fun is a neglected part of most organizations. How much fun do your people have at work? What do you do to ensure they have fun?

At every stage there's inspiration and complete equality. The person in charge of the city, the core team member, is always on the field every single day with the surveyors, moving from area to area, talking to them and solving problems on the spot. For instance, in Ahmedabad, the survey was done during summer and the surveyors were getting dehydrated. Instantly, glucose packs and water were organized for the 1000-odd surveyors even though it was not part of the plan or budget. There were several such instances of caring being displayed and problems being overcome that built huge ownership among the surveyors.

By the end of the survey period, a total of twelve lakh households had been contacted and feedback taken from them. This feedback was summarized and analysed by the core team, the editorial, reporting and feature teams and conclusions were drawn about product content and layout. Now they were ready for the equally challenging next phase that involved going back to the same households.

Think about the awesome scale of this and the 50,000-megapixel detail they go into. These guys paint a very rich canvas.

Summing Up

The Bhaskar group is a fast mover. On an average, after the decision to enter a city, Bhaskar rolls out within nine to eleven months—and reaches leadership or close to leadership position in launch after launch.

These guys are formidable, larger-than-life competitors. They moved in on Mumbai with the newspaper *DNA* though they weren't number 1 because, according to Sanjeev Kotnala, vice president and national head, MARCOM, Dainik Bhaskar group, they had made a strategic decision to enter as number 2 and grow from there. As Sanjeev says, it wasn't quite viable to be number 1 in Mumbai because to be number 1 they would have to cross five-lakh plus circulation. And given production costs, this would be a challenge. Therefore, he says, it was a strategic business decision to launch with three lakh copies, occupy a number 2 slot and grow from there. Today they are at 4.18 lakh copies in Mumbai. In the meantime, the English-language *DNA* has expanded into Ahmedabad, Surat, Pune, Jaipur and on 14 December 2008, it entered Bangalore.

Sometimes an orbit shifter doesn't need to become a leader. The job of an orbit shifter is to shift the dynamics of the industry.

Look at what these guys did systematically:

1. They set a quantum challenge to be number 2 on the day of launch, thereby challenging the long-standing industry paradigm of slow incremental growth.

2. They challenged the industry paradigm of waiting for the customer to come to them and instead went after the customers one-on-one. Lakhs of them.

3. They challenged the paradigm of the editor knowing better than the reader what the reader should read and instead involved the reader in creating his own newspaper.

4. They broke the 'impossible-to-break-morning-habit' paradigm overnight.

Today the Bhaskar group has come a long way from being number 1 in Madhya Pradesh to becoming the largest read newspaper group in the country. It now has eight titles in three languages across nine states (Madhya Pradesh, Chhattisgarh, Rajasthan, Haryana, Punjab, Himachal Pradesh, Delhi, Gujarat, Maharashtra) and the Union Territory of Chandigarh, with a mammoth 4.4 million or 44 lakh copies (approximately) being printed every day. (Note that all numbers in this chapter, except where specifically stated, are provided by the Bhaskar group.)

In the final analysis it doesn't matter who is the exact undisputed leader in X market in Y year. What matters from an orbit-shifting perspective is that here's an organization that has shown us a possibility. It has shown us that generations of collective wisdom on how to grow a newspaper brand (or any other brand) can be overturned overnight when you challenge and rethink all that has been taken for granted. And that is, perhaps, Bhaskar's greatest contribution. It has shown us, no matter what our industry, just what can be done if we only consciously seek to shift orbits.

- Decades of incremental growth can be eclipsed by six months of radical innovation. Are you part of the former or the latter? If your growth has been incremental, what are you going to do about it?
- Today, competition is no longer between products. It's between business models. Is yours radically different?
- Organizations and people often mistake the unusual for the impossible. Just because something is unusual doesn't make it impossible. Where are you mistaking the unusual for the impossible?
- Are you challenging conventional wisdom? Do you choose Krishna or His army?

3

ARAVIND EYE HOSPITAL

MAKING A DENT IN GLOBAL BLINDNESS

Steve Jobs of Apple often speaks about 'making a dent in the Universe'. But what does it take to do so? To find out, you don't have to go to Cupertino, California. Just go to tiny Madurai in Tamil Nadu. There you will find a thirty-two-year-old institution that is truly, in Jobs's words, denting the world.

Aravind Eye Hospital is internationally recognized as an institution best suited to make not just a dent, but a grand canyon in the world of blindness. There are nearly twenty-four million blind in the world. And nearly one-third of them are unnecessarily blind, which means that they don't have to stay blind; a medical intervention can treat them. But the intervention in many cases requires surgery. And there just aren't enough doctors to go around.

Instead of increasing the number of surgeons to cope with the problem of unnecessary blindness, Aravind decided to find ways to increase a surgeon's productivity. And it has perfected an assembly-line technique of surgery that increases this productivity by a factor of ten. It has also developed such a cost-effective revenue model that thousands of blind poor can be operated on for free or nearly free. Revenues are generated from a small percentage of paying patients.

What's remarkable about Aravind is that only 30 per cent of its patients pay. And that they pay less than what they would pay elsewhere. The remaining 70 per cent are treated free or almost free. The remarkable becomes astounding when you realize that this is not a small mom-and-pop charity establishment. It's a full-fledged business that makes a 35 per cent operating profit (all profits are ploughed back into expansion, as Aravind is a not-for-profit institution), treats 2.4 million outpatients and does 286,000 cataract surgeries every year. This makes it by far the largest ophthalmological institution in the world. It is also one of the most respected, with students from Harvard, John Hopkins, Yale et al coming to it for training and exposure.

Aravind follows a unique business model. It takes its inspiration from STD-booth owners and Xerox-machine operators. Both these small businesses make money on numbers while serving the community's need for such services. The unit profit margin is low. But this is made up through enormous volumes. Aravind's business feeds on a virtuous cycle. The more surgeries Aravind does, the more effective it becomes. And the more effective it becomes, the more its reputation grows, bringing in more patients—paying or otherwise.

How did a small-town hospital in one of the quietest corners of India become such a global lighthouse?

Beginning with a Dream

It all began, as most world-denting projects do, with a dream: to eliminate unnecessary blindness in India. This was the dream of

> This was not the dream of a government body or of a large powerful organization. Somehow these entities rarely seem to have dreams ... they have targets and deliverables and strategies ... *but no dreams.*

a frail, retired professor of ophthalmology at Madurai Medical College.

Dr Govindappa Venkataswamy, or Dr V, as he is called, wanted to be a gynaecologist after three of his cousins died in childbirth at a young age. But just as he was starting off his career, he fell ill and was bedridden for two years with crippling rheumatoid arthritis. Many thought he would never walk again, much less be a surgeon. But this remarkable man not only left his bed, he also slowly, inch by painful inch, taught himself surgery all over again.

As Dr V's fingers were crippled, the usual surgeon's instruments were of no use to him. He had to devise instruments specially for himself so that he could hold them. He realized he couldn't do the heavy surgical work required in gynaecology but rather than give up and sink into despair, he took up ophthalmology and went back to medical school. After graduating, he joined government service and then went into teaching. Treating unnecessary blindness became a passion with him. As a professor, he, along with his students and colleagues, pioneered rural eye camps in India. His team would go into villages around Madurai and operate on people who had lost their sight due to cataract.

While engaged in this, Dr V realized that he was doing more than just restoring sight. He was literally extending the lifespan of those he treated. In those days, a blind, elderly person was considered a mouth with no hands and was not looked after too well. As a result, life expectancy after blindness was only around two to three years. And cataract-induced blindness was literally a death sentence. With Dr V's surgeries and the restoration of sight, these people went on to live productive lives for many more years.

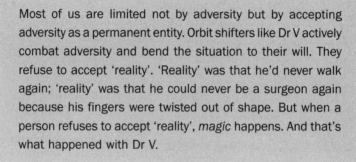

Most of us are limited not by adversity but by accepting adversity as a permanent entity. Orbit shifters like Dr V actively combat adversity and bend the situation to their will. They refuse to accept 'reality'. 'Reality' was that he'd never walk again; 'reality' was that he could never be a surgeon again because his fingers were twisted out of shape. But when a person refuses to accept 'reality', *magic* happens. And that's what happened with Dr V.

When Dr V retired in 1976 at the age of fifty-six, rather than seeing it as the end of his working life, he saw it as a beginning. He decided to set up a hospital to treat unnecessary blindness and asked his sister, Dr Natchiar, and her husband, Dr Nam, both ophthalmologists, to join him. They were then at Harvard, and were not too keen to come back, says Dr Natchiar. But Dr V was very persuasive. He was also Dr Natchiar's elder brother, had raised her after their father passed away, was her teacher in medical school and someone both she and Dr Nam respected enormously. Saying no wasn't easy. Also, the couple were concerned about Dr V. What would he do after retirement? He was a man of strong will, very disciplined, very restless. How would he stay occupied?

They decided to go along with Dr V on the journey he was proposing: to build an alternate eye care model to the government's, one that supported the government yet was not dependent on it, and one that reached the common villager. It would be community-oriented, cost-effective and world-class in quality. As Dr Natchiar says, 'We came back, but reluctantly. We thought then that we were making a great sacrifice.'

They decided to start in Madurai, where Dr V had lived and worked for fifteen years. Also, Madurai was an old town with many villages nearby, and they wanted to make a difference in rural India. And the aspiration was to eliminate unnecessary blindness in India.

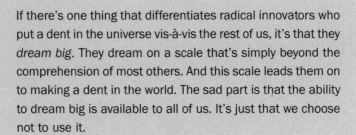

If there's one thing that differentiates radical innovators who put a dent in the universe vis-à-vis the rest of us, it's that they *dream big*. They dream on a scale that's simply beyond the comprehension of most others. And this scale leads them on to making a dent in the world. The sad part is that the ability to dream big is available to all of us. It's just that we choose not to use it.

Following the Dream

The trio needed funding to begin this dream project. People had been telling them that there would be many who would come forward for such a good cause. Indeed, they thought that it wouldn't be too difficult to raise the money. But they were mistaken. And they were embarrassed. Nobody helped, and potential lenders were not willing to give them even a hearing. The last straw came when a bank clerk told Dr V, 'You are already retired. Why do you want to burden the young people who work with you, as they would be responsible for paying back the loan if anything happened to you.' They decided then that they would never ask anyone for a loan again.

They began with an eleven-bed hospital in the house of Dr V and Dr Natchiar's brother, G. Srinivasan, after mortgaging jewellery to buy equipment. The initial years were hard. As Dr Natchiar says, 'We had problems raising the money and felt we had made a mistake in coming back. Compared to the US, where we had a car, a house and an easier life, here we had nothing and worked eighteen hours a day.' Each case was important. The paid ones netted them between Rs 2,000 and Rs 3,000 and they needed this money to sustain their eye camps.

> The difficulties in embarking on a new initiative are often so great and the initial rewards so poor that there is always the temptation to fall back upon the status quo. It needs a radical challenge or an impossible aspiration to keep people going. People persist when they believe they're making the impossible happen or doing something that's 'insanely great'.

In a few years, Dr Nam's sister and her husband joined Drs V, Natchiar and Nam. And the pool of doctors grew to five. They began to construct a hospital. Each day's earnings were ploughed back into the hospital to pay for construction or salaries. Dr V's brother, G. Srinivasan, an engineer, took charge of the construction and the finances. He ran a tight ship, juggling payments and earnings as they came in. And Aravind began its journey of constant growth, achieving the following milestones along the way:

1977: built a building with thirty beds;

1978: built a low-cost hospital with a hundred beds;

1980: moved into its present facility at Madurai (only partially completed then);

1982: present facility expanded to 200 beds and three operating rooms;

1984: free hospital set up with 400 beds and three operating rooms;

1985: Aravind Hospital at Theni set up;

1988: Aravind Hospital at Tirunelveli set up for 135 paying and 400 free patients;

1991: facility at Madurai expanded to accommodate 280 paying and 1100 free patients;

1992: Aurolab set up;

1996: Lions Aravind Institute of Community Ophthalmology (LAICO) set up;

1997: Aravind, Coimbatore, set up;

1999: hostel for PG doctors set up;

2001: free hospital expanded to accommodate another 400 patients;

2001: nurses' residential quarters set up;

2003: Aravind, Pondicherry, set up;

2004: outpatient clinic at Melur in Madurai district started, now expanded to four outpatient clinics at Thirumangalam, Tuticorin and Tirupur;

2005: vision centre serving a rural population of 50,000 piloted, this has grown to thirty vision centres at present;

2007: new state-of-the-art manufacturing facility inaugurated, manufacturing intraocular lenses, sutures, blades and pharmaceutical products used in eye care;

2007: Aravind Managed Eye Care Service (AMECS) Division started to manage eye hospitals in other parts of the country; (Aravind works with other eye hospitals in association with selected partners. They currently have four hospitals: two in Uttar Pradesh, one in Kolkata and one in Gujarat.)

2008: Dr G. Venkataswamy Eye Research Institute, a new state-of-the-art research facility, inaugurated to conduct research in molecular biology, genetic disorders in eyes and proteomic (the protein component in genes) studies.

Through all this, the Aravind philosophy and model were maturing. In order to grow, stretching mentally, physically and materially to the maximum became a way of life at Aravind. Camps were conducted on shoestring budgets; they operated for ten hours at a stretch.

With money so tight, as Dr Natchiar explains, they were constantly reducing costs, and standardization was the way to do this. They standardized everything—systems, departments, equipment, services. Today, all five hospitals have the same equipment, services and processes, which means a higher interchangeability and easier maintenance. When machines break down, parts can be transferred from one hospital to another, technicians can handle equipment at any hospital. Even nurses can be transferred anywhere and fit right in because everything is standardized. The impact of this standardization and relentless focus on costs is that Aravind, according to Dr Natchiar, is run at one-fifth the cost of similar hospitals.

> How often do we say 'if only'? If only we had the money or the resources or the people or the opportunity or the freedom ... The shocking fact is that much less of all this is needed than we think. Some of the biggest breakthroughs come about simply because the innovators faced a lack of resources—and that forced them to think differently. The lack of resources forced them to ask 'what if' instead of 'if only'.

Elaborating, Dr Natchiar says, 'We developed the philosophy that the content is more important than the container. Don't focus on the packaging. Remove all unnecessary trims.' And yet, this didn't mean a compromise on quality. The quality would be truly world-class. They used the best lenses, equipment and instruments. But anything else was pared down. Rooms were functional ... nothing that could add to expense. As Dr Natchiar puts it, 'We learnt that money is not very important in building an institution. If we had waited for the money, it might never have come. Instead, we just began and the money followed.'

In our experience, one of the prime differentiators of orbit shifters is that they just begin. They are more action oriented than planning oriented. This doesn't mean that they don't plan, it's just that they don't spend too much time waiting for 'favourable conditions'. They begin and the favourable conditions follow. The right time is right now and the best team is the one you already have. Everything else is an excuse to put off the important.

When Dr Natchiar says that the quality is world-class, she means it. Aravind goes beyond the tyranny of the 'or'. For them it is never quality or low price, this or that, price or performance. There is never an inherent compromise. It must be both: quality *and* low price. They come from a non-compromise or value-additive mindset that constantly focuses on asking what they can do for their 'customers' that's world-class. And they find ways of making that happen.

Take the case of the Intraocular Lens (IOL). When this lens first appeared, Dr V wanted it for his patients in keeping with his commitment to provide world-class eye care. IOLs cut down on postoperative recovery time and also gave infinitely better sight to cataract patients as compared to the traditional lens.

The lenses were prohibitively expensive, though. At $100 each, they were way out of most Aravind patients' budgets. Dr V and his team decided to manufacture them in-house. They had no idea about the technology, the equipment or the process. But they decided to go ahead anyway! And Aurolab was conceived.

They roped in partners to make this happen and a number of voluntary eye care institutions came in—the Seva Foundation, the Sight Savers International, and the Combat Blindness Foundation, to name a few. It became a cause. The technology was obtained from an American company with a one-time fee for technology transfer. Aravind now manufactures around 1.2 million lenses a year. Non-profit organizations receive the lenses at $4 a lens and for-profit organizations pay $8. Since its inception in 1992, Aurolab has supplied more than 6 million lenses to non-profit users in India and eighty-five other countries. Today, one in ten users of IOL across the globe uses Aurolab's lenses. Prices of IOL have crashed worldwide thanks to Aravind.

In addition to lenses, Aurolab also manufactures sutures used in cataract and eye surgery. Its cost is one-fourth the price of imported sutures. A pharmaceutical division has also been set up that manufactures the medicines required in surgery and other eye-related needs at a low cost. It currently manufactures twenty-six types of ophthalmic drops. Further, unbreakable lightweight plastic spectacle lenses are now finished at Aurolab. Aravind's

Every time Aravind wanted to do something, they went for the maximum. Intent drove strategy. The intent was always to provide world-class services nearly free. Beyond a broad idea of what they wanted to do, they had no idea how to do it. Yet they just began. The most exceptional people we know are the ones who kept going when the others quit; the ones who found ways to do what everyone else thought couldn't be done. They don't just hold down a job or do a business. They reach deep inside and find something more. They always make a difference.

patients were denied the benefits of these earlier because of the higher cost of plastic lenses. Aurolab is now an independent profit centre that provides nearly 200 per cent return on capital employed.

Aravind spends a great deal of time and effort in ensuring that its people are the best. Dr Natchiar heads HR at Aravind and, she says, there is little supervision there. 'When a person is hired, giving them an orientation and putting them in the right group is our responsibility. We hire very carefully. And I personally recruit everyone—from a doctor to a sweeper. And we spend a lot of time on selection.'

For example, Aravind's paramedical staff are the key to the success of its business model. The girls are recruited from villages and just need to have passed the tenth standard. They are trained intensively for two years and then placed as nurses. They multitask from patient preparation to nursing to patient counselling. The girls are also placed in Aurolabs and produce IOL lenses, sutures, needles, medicines and dyes for surgery. Initially, the salary is quite low at Rs 2000 per month but they get tremendous satisfaction from helping people regain their sight and earn respect and recognition in the community.

This is one of Aravind's breakthrough innovations. It's a win-win arrangement—Aravind gets affordable, dedicated manpower, and the nurses get a good job as well as tremendous respect in society. Aravind has also challenged the establishment in doing this. All Indian nurses have to be graduates and have to have passed a nursing examination. Aravind decided to set up its own syllabus and training and to recruit those who have passed the tenth standard.

The screening and selection of paramedical staff thus becomes very important. And Drs Natchiar and Usha spend a lot of time on this. They meet the girls along with their parents to understand the family. They talk about the organization as extended family.

As Dr Natchiar says, 'We don't look for intelligence; we look for common sense.' They don't ask general knowledge questions like 'Who's the prime minister,' etc. Instead, if the girl is from a farming family, they ask her questions like how much water an acre of the crop they grow requires, or what the ploughing time for an acre is. If she is able to answer these questions, it shows that she has been interested in and engaged with the family business. And this is the kind of engaged, involved person they want.

After she is selected, she is put through an orientation programme for a month. Everyone from doctors to non-clinical workers go through this programme, which highlights the heritage, the value system and the culture of Aravind. During this time, they are partnered with mentors—exceptional performers at a similar job—who act as an inspiration and inculcate the Aravind way of life into them. And, as Dr Natchiar says, 'You can see it happening. The discipline happening without anything being said—seven a.m. in, seven p.m. out. No supervision required. Every day we see about three thousand people, operate on nearly three hundred, but there's no chaos, no rush, nothing. There's an all-pervasive calmness. No yelling. This is not difficult if a system exists. But we need to mould and inspire people to stick to the system and its purpose. We don't allow them to do any task until this one-month period is over.'

The nursing or paramedical staff literally forms the backbone of Aravind as they take up a lot of what would be doctors' responsibilities in other hospitals. They do refraction testing, counselling and

Aravind hires paramedical staff with lower educational qualifications than those in other institutes, hires them from rural and backward areas and yet gives them far more responsibility than the other institutions do. And the paramedical staff deliver. It's not the education that counts ... it's the attitude, the training and the trust you put in.

help patients decide what kind of surgery/treatment to go in for, freeing the doctors' time for more surgery and medical consultation.

All the doctors at Aravind work full-time. Private practice is not allowed and there are no part-time consultants as in other hospitals. Aravind believes that this is essential to develop institutional loyalty and the work culture and necessary skills needed to make mass impact.

The training of doctors also follows a similar process at Aravind, with the focus on the organization's philosophy and way of life. They too are partnered by 'mentors' who are role models who instil the Aravind way of life in them.

THE ARAVIND WAY OF LIFE

So what is the Aravind way of life? According to Dr Nam, 'When you do something, your people will do it too and it will become a part of their lives. If they are *asked* to do something that you don't do, they will do it, but will forget it soon after. Therefore, always lead by example.'

The senior doctors are so hands-on that leading by example has become a way of life at Aravind. As Dr Nam says, 'People don't need to be told to come in early. They see us doing it day after day and they follow. When we see something dusty or dropped on the floor, we clean it or pick it up. They see us doing it and do the same themselves.' Of course, the Aravind way of life is also about constantly stretching oneself and going after the next horizon.

It is this way of life and philosophy that makes the Aravind model quite hard to replicate. Aravind is very open and transfers its knowledge of hospital management systems across the world. But as Dr Natchiar says, 'The difficulty lies in transferring the inner spirit and attitude. We can show them the cost measures, the systems, the administration details, the marketing, the standardization ... everything but the inner spirit.' People pick up the processes, the methods, the structures but not the 'inner spirit' or the Aravind way of life. The tangible 'hardware' is picked up but not the intangible 'software'. And in an organization of low supervision yet high impact, it's this software that is critical.

Orbit shifters like the Aravind team are paradoxes in many ways: gentle people, but slave drivers who motivate by example. They care deeply for team members yet push them to the limits ... and then push them further. They tend to stretch people and enable them to achieve impossible goals.

> What do *your* people believe they are doing? Drop dead boring work or something that makes a *real* difference? What are they doing that's 'insanely great'? What can you do to cause that feeling?

The Famous Assembly Line

In the 1950s and 60s, Dr V was grappling with the issue of scale as he realized just how monumental the task of eradicating needless blindness was. In 1961, he started his eye camps. He and his team of doctors would travel hundreds of kilometres deep into rural Tamil Nadu and diagnose patients and conduct cataract surgeries there. But the impact seemed very small. If they had to eliminate cataract as a cause for blindness, doctors had to do many more operations than they were currently doing. Around this time, he went to the US and encountered McDonald's restaurants with their assembly line operations and standardizations. Here, he realized, was a breakthrough proposition. He was convinced that this technique could make a radical difference to blindness if he could find a way to marry the two—surgery and McDonald's. He did. And if the figures are anything to go by, it did make a radical difference. An average ophthalmologist operates on 250 to 400 patients a year. An Aravind ophthalmologist using the McDonald's-inspired assembly line technique operates on 2000 patients a year.

At Aravind, the day starts at 7 a.m. for doctors. Nurses come in at 6.30 a.m. and prepare the patients for the day. Patients are scheduled for each doctor. By 7.15 a.m., two patients are on two adjacent operating tables. One operation theatre has four operating tables laid side by side and two surgeons handle these four tables.

In our experience, the ability to marry principles and ideas from two diverse fields is one of the unique characteristics of radical innovators. They constantly *trawl* the world for ideas and look across diverse fields to see what can be applied back at work. What ideas and techniques are you consciously trawling the world for? Are you fixated only on your own industry?

In many hospitals, keeping two patients in the operating theatre is not allowed because of the risk of infection. But Aravind challenged this as its patients are mostly healthy and come in only for eye surgery. Therefore, the risk of infection is low. Its low rates of postoperative complications bear this out. Based on research by the Royal College of Ophthalmologists, Aravind's postoperative complications are lower on many comparable parameters than for hospitals in the UK.

Each patient has two nurses. One assists the doctor, and the other, called a running nurse, brings surgical instruments from a sterilization area about twenty-five metres away. Each doctor operates with two assisting nurses and two running nurses. This comparatively large team is one key reason why doctors perform so many more surgeries at Aravind than anywhere else in the world.

By the time the surgeon finishes with one patient, the other one on the adjacent table is ready with the microscope focused on the eye to be operated on. The operated patient is moved out and the third one is brought in and kept in operational readiness. The moment the surgeon finishes with the second patient, he swivels to the third with minimal loss of time and effort. He constantly moves between the tables with barely a break. It's quite common for each surgeon to do about twenty-five to thirty surgeries between 7 a.m. and 1 p.m. There are no operations in the afternoon and the theatre is scrubbed and kept ready for the next day's surgeries. The surgeons spend the rest of the day in either outpatient work or research.

This process has ensured that Aravind's surgeons do many, many more surgeries than any eye surgeon across the globe. The elite medical schools of the globe come to Aravind to study its methods.

THE DYNAMICS OF NEXT-HORIZON THINKING

What is striking about Aravind is that everyone there from Dr V to Drs Natchiar, Nam, Usha to Dr Aravind, the administrator, all talk about the next horizon.

Aravind Eye Hospital is currently doing 286,000 surgeries a year. Dr Aravind talks about scaling this to one million by 2015. Dr Nam talks about eradicating diabetic-related blindness in another ten years, despite the fact that India, according to Dr Aravind, has around 42 million diabetics, of which about 20 per cent tend to suffer from diabetes-related blindness. That's about eight million people requiring intervention! Dr V talks about using IT and rural internet connectivity to bring in more patients. Both Dr V and Dr Nam talk about the fact that only 7 per cent of those requiring eye care see a doctor. What's happening to the other 93 per cent? The doctors are constantly focused on ways of getting this vast number into the treatment loop.

The entire organization is obsessed with the next horizon. The ambition now is to reach a *billion* people.

The Lions Aravind Institute of Community Ophthalmology (LAICO) is an offshoot of Aravind's next-horizon thinking. As part of its crusade to eradicate needless blindness globally, Aravind shares its processes and methods with anyone who wants to learn. In 1992, in collaboration with Lions International, it set up LAICO. Groups and institutions from across the world come to LAICO to learn Aravind's replicable model of mass eye care.

The objective of LAICO is to improve the planning, efficiency and effectiveness of eye hospitals across the world with a special focus on developing countries. It teaches, trains, researches and consults. It has worked with over 150 hospitals across India, Southeast Asia and Africa. LAICO offers long-term courses in hospital management and short-term courses in community outreach, social marketing and instruments maintenance. That's fission—spreading your model into every corner of the world!

What causes this next-horizon thinking?

First, the size of the mission itself. According to Dr Aravind, 'Next-horizon thinking comes from our mission—eradicating needless blindness. It's a large mission. We don't say eradicate one disease in this or that geographical region. It's broader—unnecessary blindness anywhere.'

Second, they think mission back rather than resource forward. As Dr Aravind says, 'We go behind the issue of blindness and not behind resources. We've always striven to reach people no matter what the constraints. And doing that, we found, brings in resources rather than the other way around.' According to Dr Natchiar, 'money is not very important in building an institution. If we really go after the purpose, the money will always follow.'

This uncannily echoes Goethe: 'Concerning all acts of initiative and creation ... The moment one definitely commits oneself, then providence moves too. All sorts of things occur to help one that would never otherwise have occurred ... Boldness has genius, power and magic in it. Begin it now.'

Third, there is a mindset of fluidity and expansion at Aravind. Dr V is an inspiration with his energy, his constant stretch for more, and his sharing of practices with hospitals across the globe. There's no hoarding of knowledge or information. It's all freely shared. The thrust for contacting more and more patients comes from Dr V who created a paradigm shift by refusing to wait for patients to come to him and instead actively 'sold' free services to those most in need of them.

At Aravind, everything is measured not by how much has been done but by how much remains to be done. Their aspirations have kept rising—from eliminating unnecessary blindness in India to eliminating unnecessary blindness globally. It's an aspiration like this that has placed it firmly on the global eye map. And today they are in the position to make a truly global impact. To make a difference to a billion lives!

So what's *your* excuse? If the dream of a frail old man can make a dent in the world, what's your excuse for not dreaming? Too old to do anything much? Too young to do much? Retired? Just joined? Too powerless? Too high in the hierarchy? Too low in the hierarchy? Physically incapable? Spiritually? Mentally? These are just some of the rationalizations that we dish out to others and ourselves for not maximizing our skills and talents. But look at this man ... He set up the world-famous Aravind Eye Hospital at the age of fifty-six after retiring from government service. Most of us would have sat back and 'retired'.

If there is a key lesson to draw from the Aravind story, it is that it's always possible to make a dent in the universe. It all begins with a dream—and an irreverent mindset that challenges everything and refuses to accept any situation as a given.

SECTION II

CHALLENGING THE ESTABLISHMENT THROUGH A BREAKTHROUGH INSIGHT

An orbit-shifting challenge needs an out-of-the-box strategy. When Dr V of Aravind Eye Hospital took on the orbit-shifting challenge of eliminating blindness across the world, he needed to create a completely new business model of healthcare delivery as the vast majority of the needless blind are in the poor rural areas of the country. He had to create a strategy and business model that would reduce costs dramatically and yet entail huge reach. The major constraint he faced in delivering on this business model was that, on an average, surgeons could do only four to five surgeries a day. This was too expensive a proposition. To enable his business model to succeed, he needed a breakthrough insight. He got it at McDonald's, and the McDonaldization or assembly line process of eye surgery was born. And using that insight he developed his strategy and low-cost business model.

Contrast this with the usual modes of creating strategies, which is often about trying to gauge how much a market will grow, what the trends point to, and then trying to 'fit' into the market using past performance as a guideline. Insipid to say the least! If your past has been unremarkable, why blight your future by tethering it to your past?

Most of our thinking is historical and limited to our own histories or the histories of others in our industry. Expertise has history behind it. Taking on an orbit-shifting challenge means suspending history for a while. To put a man on the moon when no one has done it before means you can't dig into history. No precedence exists.

Perhaps the largest block to breakthrough thinking is not a cognitive block. It's an emotional block. When people move beyond the emotional block of history and expertise, when they look in different directions, they come up with a breakthrough.

An out-of-box strategy needs breakthrough thinking, and there are at least three operating principles which prevent breakthrough thinking:

(i)   The operating principle of seeking precedents;
(ii)   The operating principle of stopping at the 'why it can't be done' stage;
(iii)   The operating principle of looking for insights in the same places we have always looked for them.

When the operating principle of seeking precedents kicks in, the first question is always: 'Has it been done before?' And if it hasn't been done before, it's not possible. If it were possible, somebody else would have thought of it. The mindset is one of subservience and the operating principle is one of seeking precedents.

B.G. Dwarakanath, senior vice president and business head, Precision Engineering at Titan, speaks about his earlier experiences when he was at Hindustan Machine Tools (HMT). Every time he came up with something innovative or different, the first reaction of his bosses, who had spent eighteen months at Japan with their technical partner Citizen, was: 'If even the Japanese haven't done it, it can't be possible. Therefore drop it.' And when Dwarakanath finally went behind their backs and sent across a radical idea to Citizen, the Japanese reverted saying they would like to team up with him in developing this brilliant new technology.

The mindset that achieves this is that of the explorer and the operating principle is one of: 'Find a way or create one.' Just because a roadmap doesn't exist doesn't mean it can't be done. Rajiv Narang of Erehwon goes in with an operating principle of 'It's not undoable. It's just that an idea hasn't yet been found'. And as he says, he feels a great sense of discomfort till he finds a solution. Kunwer Sachdev of Su-Kam has a simple operating principle: 'Jo sabne kiya woh nahin karna. Naya kya kar sakte hain?' (We won't do anything that everyone else in the industry is doing. What can we do that's different?)

The second operating principle that prevents breakthrough thinking is the principle of stopping at what I call Level-1 thinking. Stopping at the 'Why it can't be done' stage. But breakthrough thinking needs something to break through. And that means going to Level-2 thinking, to the 'how it can be done' stage. The operating principle here that enables breakthrough is: 'Move from why it can't be done to how it can be done.' G.K. Prasanna, who heads Wipro's Remote Infrastructure Services, has a simple operating principle: 'If something is not possible it only means a tool doesn't yet exist. Create the tool and the impossible becomes possible.' And using this principle, Wipro and Prasanna became pioneers in Remote Infrastructure Services where they manage infrastructure in the US and Europe from half a world away in India.

The third operating principle that prevents breakthrough thinking is the principle of looking for ideas in the same places we have always looked. But if there's an orbit-shifting challenge, we need orbit-shifting ideas. And if we look in the same places we have always looked, we won't find them. As Carsten of Arla Foods, who worked on an out-of-the-box challenge to put milk into space, says, 'We created a challenge so strong that it pulled the team out of gravity, making them do things differently from the way they normally thought. The challenge was so much stronger than what they normally did that even the dullest team member thought "Wow! I have to do something different and the metrics that I normally work with may not apply here." We needed to look at a completely different area for packaging for space—like perhaps use dispensers, or perhaps pack milk like sausages. Somebody somewhere is solving similar problems. We need to look in a different direction.'

Here's what people from a leading international pharmaceutical company had to say about seeking insights: 'We use the same insight sources as others in pharma. We work with an external agency and give them a brief. They do qualitative research and uncover ideas that we then elaborate and test. Testing is again through an agency doing further qualitative tests (meeting with doctors, customers etc). We use similar market research companies as others. It's not surprising we all look alike.'

For breakthrough thinking there is a need to look in a different place. For example, a company wanted to understand why Indian women don't go in for permanent hair removal. To understand this they spoke to the usual suspects—dermatologists. Nothing much was emerging, until Devika Deviah at Erehwon suggested that they needed to look in a different direction. They then reframed the question to ask: where else has something that was about permanence moved from the periphery to mainstream? That led them to tattoos. They spoke to tattoo artists and those who have got tattoos to understand the movement to mainstream, and some very interesting insights emerged.

The operating principle that overcomes this is 'scan the peripheries and the intersections' versus 'dig deeper into the existing and usual areas'. Somebody somewhere is dealing with your challenge in a different industry. For instance, after 9/11, the US army realized they had no clue about how to deal with terror strikes. They were simply not trained that way. Their only source of insight was *Jane's Defence Weekly*. They then began roping in

Hollywood scriptwriters and directors who had scripted just such an attack in a movie a couple of years before it actually happened. They now scan the intersections and peripheries instead of just digging deeper into *Jane's Defence Weekly*.

The mindset to creating an out-of-the-box strategy is really one of seeking first-hand insight. Insights cannot be outsourced. They have to be garnered first-hand. Every orbit shifter we know is very hands-on in the sense that he goes to the field personally to garner insights. C.K. Ranganathan, MD of CavinKare, personally goes to the field for insight dialogues before any meeting with his executive team. Sivakumar of ITC-IBD does the same. A.G. Lafley, the head of the century-old Proctor and Gamble, regularly goes to the field all over the world to pick up insights. He credits a lot of his company's innovations to the fact that he and his management team go out for first-hand insight. Where do your strategies emerge from? Do they come from the boardroom or from the field?

The three orbit-shifting missions we discuss in this section— CavinKare, ITC-IBD and Bosch India—created new businesses around out-of-the-box strategies. And the head of each business regularly goes to the field for first-hand insight that enables him to continually develop his strategy. To paraphrase Todd Skinner, when you journey off the map, what you know is less important than how you think and where you get your inputs from.

4

CAVINKARE

GIVING GIANTS COLDS

In Southeast Asia they say that when Hindustan Lever sneezes in India, Unilever share prices across Asia catch a cold. And perhaps the one person who has made Hindustan Lever sneeze the most number of times is C.K. Ranganathan of CavinKare.

It takes radical innovators to make giants catch colds. And C.K. Ranganathan, who started CavinKare in 1983 with a seed capital of just Rs 15,000, has a record of giving colds to transnational FMCG giants.

How do you make giants worth billions blink when you have just Rs 15,000 to play with? The answer is simple: You level the playing field. And *insight* is one of the greatest levellers of playing fields, for insights trigger innovation.

Across the world, insights level giants. Lenovo computers of China had the insight that most Chinese buy computers for connecting to the internet but then get frustrated as they face connectivity problems. Lenovo came up with internet-ready computers that could access the net with a single button. And they emerged market leaders. Eventually, IBM, once their biggest competitor, sold out to them.

CavinKare's Ranganathan, too, has based his company's strategy on cutting-edge consumer insight. Beginning with a capital of Rs 15,000, he has grown his business to Rs 725 crore—all from internal accruals. In 2004, *The Economic Times* voted Ranganathan 'Entrepreneur of the Year', stating, 'C.K. Ranganathan emerged the winner due to the fact that it [CavinKare] is a small company, has built a solid brand, has rewritten the rules of the game in the FMCG market, has touched the pulse of the small consumer with affordable good quality products and forced the biggest industry players to follow suit and make products affordable to the smallest consumer.'

A TAXING INITIATION

It all started in 1983, when Ranga left his family business, Velvette, and branched out on his own. Velvette had pioneered the sachet marketing revolution in India. Ranga branched off by setting up Beauty Cosmetics (later renamed CavinKare) and introduced Chik shampoo sachets.

The beginnings were truly challenging. As Ranga says, he rented a house-cum-office for Rs 250 a month against an advance of Rs 1000 and factory space for Rs 300 a month against an advance of Rs 1200. He then bought a shampoo-packing machine for Rs 3000.

He named his product Chik Shampoo, after his father, Chinni Krishan. It took him three years to get the first loan because banks asked for collateral and he did not have any. But one particular bank gave him a loan of Rs 25,000, which he rotated and upgraded to Rs 4 lakh and then Rs 15 lakh.

Ranga says he got the loan because the bank manager wrote

in his loan application: 'This person does not have any collateral to offer but there is something interesting about this Small Scale Industry unit. Unlike others, this company pays income tax!' As Ranga would tell Rediff News later, 'I must say my business never looked back because I was very particular about paying income tax.'

Money was tight and, initially, he used to struggle to pay his suppliers on time. But soon, he says, he was able to develop a very good relationship with his suppliers. In his words, 'I was struggling initially because of the low capital. I appointed one representative and carefully rotated the capital. Two, three times you pay the supplier on time, they will have more confidence in you. It is one of the fundamentals, and once you win them over, they are ready to help. I am thankful to them.'

With the supply in place, the next step was to stabilize the marketing network. In creating his marketing network, Ranga decided to change the norms. He did not enter into arrangements with established players; rather, he invited stockists who had no prior experience in selling FMCG products. His logic for hiring 'freshmen' was that (i) since they were starting out, they would be willing to work on his terms; and (ii) experience in this business did not matter. What mattered was that they should have fire in the belly, and a strong desire to come up in life. In fact, experience might even be a disabler when it comes to doing things differently. Those with experience are more used to certain kinds of engagement norms, both at a financial and at a relationship level.

Initially, progress was slow. In 1983, Chik India clocked an annual turnover of Rs 5 lakhs. However, by 1986, things seemed to be stabilizing for Ranga and Chik India started clocking an average turnover of Rs 2.5 to 3 lakhs per month.

The Out-of-the-Box Strategy

In spite of this, the one thing that constantly bothered Ranga was that his shampoo was not the one that had the highest market recall. The feedback he received kept telling him that when consumers thought of packet shampoo, the first thing that came to mind was Velvette—the company he had left, and not Chik. This got Ranga thinking: how would consumers come back again and again and ask for Chik?

To address this problem, in 1988, Ranga came up with an innovative marketing idea: he would give one sachet of Chik shampoo free for every four empty sachets of any shampoo that people brought back to the retailer. This scheme was the first of its kind and it took the market by storm. Later, he changed the scheme and began giving one free sachet of Chik shampoo for every four used Chik sachets. Initially, his colleagues told him that the retailers were misusing the offer. For instance, they were collecting empty sachets dropped on the road and getting a new one in exchange. However, Ranga kept the idea alive as, in his view, in spite of the misuse, consciously or unconsciously, consumer momentum for Chik was picking up.

Ranga was right. The one-for-four offer proved to be a huge success and, consequently, contributed to a significant increase in the sales volumes for Chik India. The recall value for Chik shampoos was at an all-time high and Chik was no longer just another commodity—it was now a brand. Sales went up to Rs 12 lakhs a month from around Rs 3 lakhs in just a month. By 1990-91, Chik had an annual turnover of Rs 400 lakhs and it had become the second-largest selling shampoo in Tamil Nadu behind Velvette.

By 1992, Chik had become the largest-selling shampoo in Tamil Nadu with a turnover of Rs 8 crores, and by 1993, Ranga was ready to go national. A few years later, Chik became for a time the largest-selling sachet shampoo in the country. It's now a close number two to the leader—Clinic Plus. Chik's explosive growth came when Ranga began honing his 'insighting' skills.

CHIC INSIGHTS

With 72 per cent of India's population living in rural areas and only 8 per cent penetration of shampoos there, shampoos were, largely, an urban phenomenon in India. As Ranga says, there was nearly a 70 per cent awareness of shampoos in the rural market, but low usage. The total penetration of shampoos in India was only 14 per cent. So what did the remaining 86 per cent use? Ranga decided to find out.

The major shifts happened when Ranga met some consumers around Chennai and asked them one-on-one about what they used for their hair. They said, 'Soap.' Ranga was curious. Why did they use soap? Didn't they know it was bad for hair? In one such conversation, a man said that Ranga was biased since he was from a shampoo company and wanted to sell shampoos. And that was why he was saying that soap was bad. His father and grandfather had used soap all their lives and nothing had happened to them. His grandfather still had a thick shock of hair in his seventies. So how could soap be bad?

Ranga realized that short of demonstrating through a microscope, he couldn't really explain how soap harmed the hair. He had an insight: if a consumer believes strongly in something, don't attack it; he won't believe you. Instead, find the barriers to their using your product.

His rural market strategy, like that of other companies, was till then based on his sales teams going around in rural areas, gathering people and 'educating' them about the disadvantages of using soap and the advantages of using shampoos. He realized that, for so many years, they might have been wasting their collective breaths.

Instead of repeating this mistake, Ranga asked another question: 'What makes it difficult for you to use shampoo?' It emerged that price was the most important barrier. Shampoo bottles were prohibitively expensive, but even sachets cost between one and two rupees. Rural families typically have five to six members. For a family of six to wash their hair once a week at Rs 2 a wash, it would cost Rs 12 a week. That worked out to nearly Rs 50 per month. Far too high for a rural family in the 1980s.

An insight can show you how your current strategy and that of your industry is off track. At first thought, it's obvious and logical to 'educate' people about the evils of soap if they use soaps instead of shampoos. Many brand managers talk about 'educating' the dumb customer. With so many brands around, each one bent on educating you, one might as well go live in a classroom. When Ranga drilled down and asked the question, 'What prevents you from using shampoo?' he got the real reason: price. The consumer didn't need education—in fact that was backfiring. He needed a small enough unit price.

So the next question was: what price would excite you? Twenty-five-paise a sachet would really excite, but even fifty paise was good enough. At fifty paise, the same family's hair washing costs would drop to Rs 12 a month!

Ranga went back to his team and began discussing the possibility of selling shampoos at a fifty-paisa price point. Chik already existed at Re 1. The brand, sales and finance teams thought that selling at fifty paise would mean 'cutting their own feet' as the Re 1 sachet would stop selling. It would be (horrors!) cannibalized.

———❦———

We have found that the one thing that takes organizations rapidly down the path of diminishing returns and frozen innovation is the fear of cannibalization. Organizations are so petrified of cannibalization that it seems they would rather keep themselves open to outsider innovators coming in to capture the entire market rather than cannibalize their own products.

What's so sacrosanct about your product anyway? Instead of going for another product developed by the company which can get a larger market share over all, most organizations focus on market segmentation. They slice, dice, cube, minimize markets so much that finally it's a wonder any part of the market is left standing. What about the big picture? What about grabbing the entire market? And that means not just the existing buyers, but also all those who have never bought the product before. When we operate from a scarcity mindset, we see the market as limited to a fixed number of buyers. When we operate from an abundance mindset, the whole world is your market. There's just no need for segmentation.

———❦———

Ranga and his team were in a dilemma over whether to go ahead or not. At a gut level, Ranga felt that once people had bought his sachet at Re 1, they would not go down to fifty paise. His idea was to make the fifty-paisa sachet at half the volume of the Re 1 sachet but at a concentrate that could deliver value equal to Re 1. The size perception would make the Re 1 consumer feel that it was a small size, and therefore not for him. The existing consumers would, he believed, continue with the Re 1 sachet, while hordes of new customers, who were earlier locked out, would come in at the fifty-paisa price point. So he took a call and decided to go ahead with selling at fifty paise in 1998. As he says, they wanted to increase sales. They could wait for the economy to go up and then sell more Re 1 shampoos, or take a risk and expand the market by making the product available at a mass price. They decided on the latter.

> How often have you heard this: 'We can't grow because the market isn't growing.' When Ranga was asked during a market slump how he'd manage growth in a downturn, he replied, 'What downturn? I have 10 per cent of the market. Hindustan Lever has 90 per cent. That's my market. Where's the downturn?'

Actualizing the Insight

Now that they had decided to launch at fifty paise, they had to figure out a way to do it. It was a huge challenge to drop the price by 50 per cent. The R&D people threw up their hands saying it was not possible to reduce costs that much without compromising on quality. But as Ranga says, the biggest block to growth is the term 'not possible'. Once you say something is not possible it stops you from thinking further. And the R&D team stopped thinking further. They began shaking their heads every time the new price was mentioned. Ranga, who has a background in chemistry, actually had to roll up his sleeves and get involved in the reformulation along with his colleagues. They worked out various innovative methods of formulation, focusing on cost and quality at the same time. Finally they managed it, and the fifty-paisa shampoo was born.

As Ranga puts it, 'Size and volume wise, the fifty-paisa pack at 4 ml was half that of the Re 1 pack, but could deliver in terms of wash exactly like the one-rupee pack as we just removed excess water and made it a concentrate. By making it in a different size we made both packs coexist and grow aggressively. The fifty-paisa pack became the recruiter and after some time the consumer upgraded to Re 1. We improved the Re 1 shampoo to deliver more conditioning and fragrance so that the upgraded consumer was happy with his decision and stayed at the new price point.'

Ranga went a step further. A 50-ml bottle of shampoo typically costs twice as much as a sachet of the same volume. So if six 8-ml sachets cost Rs 6, a bottle of 50 ml would typically cost Rs 10–15. This was primarily because of government levies that pushed costs of bottles up. But rather than accept the situation, Ranga decided to do something about it. As he says, sachets get over fast and if a family forgets to buy them, they will forgo them and use soap instead, thus reducing consumption. He needed to keep shampoo available at homes at all times. Therefore, he brought out a 50-ml bottle at Rs 6! And this bottle captured an additional 5 per cent market share.

With the fifty-paisa sachet and the Rs 6 bottle, Ranga's prediction of market expansion came true. Chik tapped a huge untapped market and its market share increased from 5 per cent to 22 per cent within two years by 2000–01. Today, it's the second-largest selling shampoo in the country behind Clinic Plus.

Prototyping with Further Insights

Insight has been the key to Ranga's success as an entrepreneur and it has enabled him to take on competitors with much deeper pockets, advertising budgets and marketing muscle. With insights, Ranga levels the playing field. As he says, learning about the consumer only through market research—which is what his competitors do—is like learning to drive by reading the instruction manual.

Ranga next set about trying to find an answer to the question, 'What do the 82 per cent of Indians who don't use shampoo do for hair care?' He found that a sizeable percentage, in addition to using soap, used traditional natural products like shikakai etc. This led Ranga to another idea: Could he leverage this already existing Indian habit of using natural products? Each state in India seemed to use natural products that were unique to it, while there were some that were common across states. For instance, in Andhra he found that people used 'reetha' nuts. Could he manufacture a reetha nut-based shampoo?

Through insight dialogues he found that apart from reetha, people considered badam (almond) to be very important for hair nourishment. Ranga then created a shampoo, Meera, which combined both reetha and badam. It was an instant success, and sells at a premium.

Since then he has launched Meera with shikakai in Tamil Nadu, as shikakai is associated with hair nourishment there. He has launched Meera with hibiscus leaves in Kerala, and in Karnataka, he has launched a low-cost version under the brand name Karthika (with a mixture of herbs that are preferred by the people of Karnataka for hair care)—a second brand that retails at Re 1 while Meera sells at Rs 2.

Because of these initiatives, CavinKare is the largest overall hair wash company in south India. Hindustan Unilever (HUL) and P&G are behind them. According to Ranga, in Andhra they have a market share of 48 per cent and in Tamil Nadu over 43 per cent. In Karnataka, too, they are higher than HUL and P&G.

And the insights continued, as Ranga decided to check out the perfume market.

The perfume market is a small one with a penetration of less than 1 per cent. During customer dialogues, he found that almost everyone said he/she used perfume. But on digging further, he found that the consumer typically used it very sparingly—only on occasions like weddings or functions. Further, people preserve perfume, keeping it carefully locked up in cupboards to prevent other family members from using it. Perfumes were thus saved and stored for years. They were treated as scarce resources even in middle-class families.

Ranga kept prototyping in real time. He did a limited launch, let customers use the product, got feedback, made a change, went back again, and again. He keeps going back to the customer with product versions. That's one of the key differentiators of radical innovators. They don't launch with an all-or-nothing mindset. They launch with a versioning mindset. They make prototype after prototype and keep maturing the product. It's never frozen in time. And with every launch they gather insights that help them further mature the product. Take, for instance, the fact that consumers prefer a small glass vial to plastic or a pouch. This insight may never have come about unless the product was first put into the market. Or the fact that perfume has to last all day. Most dialogue is around the aroma. Rarely about the duration of the aroma. But prototypes tend to throw up these kinds of insights. Prototyping is one of the highest forms of insighting. Only when they have a physical prototype in hand can clients tell us, as Michael Schrage says in *Serious Play*, 'You've given us what we asked for. But now that we've seen it, we realize that it's not what we really want.' And orbit shifters listen to them. Because that's what they are prototyping for.

What about those who said they didn't like perfume? When pressed, they said that it caused a headache. On probing further, Ranga found that the price was a barrier. A good perfume bottle cost on an average Rs 100. Therefore, these people weren't using it. Sensing an opportunity, Ranga introduced 'Spinz' at Rs 10 a pack. It did well, but Ranga wasn't happy with the response. He then introduced a Rs 2 single-use pack. The initial response was very good, but then off-takes reduced. He went back to the customer. And found that they wanted a perfume that lasted a whole day and not just for two to three hours. They also wanted perfume in a glass bottle, because that's what they had come to associate good perfume with. Ranga and his team began work on it and emerged with a cute 2-ml glass vial called 'Dabon'. For a while Spinz was the fourth-largest perfume by sales, though now, according to Ranga, it's not doing as well. But, as he says, they will persevere to make it work.

The Fairever Success

It was February 1998 and the going was good for CavinKare. All their products were leaders in their respective categories. Ranga decided that it was time to increase his product portfolio. He studied the fairness cream market and uncovered some interesting facts:

(i)   The business was one of high margins;
(ii)   It was dominated by a single player (Fair and Lovely, with over 90 per cent market share); and
(iii) The penetration levels in the business were low (only 6 per cent).

Several players had previously unsuccessfully tried to enter this business. The biggest constraint for most companies was the advertising budget. The Fair and Lovely advertising budget, for example, exceeded CavinKare's turnover! Therefore, in order to succeed, Ranga knew that he had to come up with something different, something that would break the spell that Fair and Lovely had cast on the market and encourage people to buy his product.

In order for people to buy his product, he had to achieve two things:

(i)   Build credibility in the minds of his customers; and

(ii)   Make his product appeal to them.

Ranga and his team *co-evolved* Fairever with the consumer. Instead of developing the product in-house, they decided to tap into the customers' beliefs and traditions. The result was an almost instant hit. How do you develop products and services? Do you first develop them internally and then go to the customer? What if you co-evolved the product with the customer?

CavinKare developed a fairness cream and showed it to customers. They said it was nice, but not thrilling. So Ranga and his team went on an 'insighting' pilgrimage asking customers what would be thrilling for them. What did they consider to be important ingredients for fairness? One lady mentioned that in her family, pregnant women were given saffron and milk to drink as they felt this would make the child fair and healthy.

Ranga's team explored this further and found that this was a very common belief, and that it was also backed by Ayurvedic texts. But what about external application? Did Ayurvedic texts also mention external application? They dug some more—actually a lot more—and found that sure enough, the texts mentioned that milk and saffron could be used both internally and externally. They had their product. And 'Fairever' was born.

As Ranga says, 'A fairness cream that contained saffron and

milk gave instant credibility to Fairever in the minds of the consumers. We also thought of moving away from the "fairness for marriage" position that Fair and Lovely had taken. Fairness is something that attracts people much earlier than in their early twenties (typical marriage age group), and continues to attract them even after marriage. Therefore, why not position Fairever as a cream that could help you "change your life/future"?' Ranga decided to do just this.

CavinKare's usual strategy was to price its products lower than that of its competitors. However, with Fairever, they decided to price the product at a premium. Their insights told them that customers were willing to pay more as they knew that saffron was expensive.

Another factor that worked in CavinKare's favour was the relationship that Ranga developed with the distributors. As often happens with any monopoly, its distributors and customers feel trapped no matter what the company does for them. When CavinKare entered the fray, it redefined distributor relationships by increasing the margins for them and also by recognizing their efforts through public functions (for example, there were Fairever-sponsored Ms Local Area contests, the prizes for which were given by the distributor amidst coverage by the local press). This created a great deal of ownership amongst the distributors.

With both these strategies working for CavinKare, Fairever was able to wrest up to 18 per cent market share in the first year of its introduction in south India! Today, it commands around 8 per cent market share on an all-India basis.

THE CONSTANT ENTREPRENEUR

Ranga is a serial entrepreneur. He has moved from personal products to foods with the 'Ruchi' and 'Chinni' brands of pickles.

Ranga is the quintessential orbit shifter and challenger. He is not intimidated by big business. If anything, he intimidates big business. If there's one thing that Ranga's story tells us, it's that any playing field can be leveled by using insights that lead to innovation. If Ranga can do it, so can you. Look for those insights.

He sensed an opportunity during his market visits when he saw some small enterprises selling single-use pickle sachets. These were packed in unhygienic polythene packs. When tested, all the sachets showed high levels of microbial infestation due to contact with human hands during processing and packing. CavinKare worked with machine manufacturers to develop a pickle packing machine. It is very difficult to pack pickles due to their inconsistent heterogenic form—that is, oils float separately and also each piece of lime or mango is of a different size due to inconsistencies in cutting. No such pickle packing machine existed in the market. Finally a machine was developed and also a process that could deliver zero microbial infestation. Today, Chinni is the largest-selling sachet pickle in the whole of India.

Today, CavinKare is a Rs 750 crore company. What's fascinating about CavinKare is not its growth from Rs 15,000 to Rs 750 crore, but its growth in a mix of areas. Ranga is a scrappy entrepreneur who is not afraid of taking on large MNCs on their own turf. Most local and domestic players other than Nirma have been afraid of MNCs coming after them. But here is one whose biggest turnover comes from products that take on MNCs head-on. His best results come not from finding new uncontested spaces to enter, but by taking on MNCs in their established spaces—and winning through insight. He uses insight to carve a space for himself in a market crowded with big international players. As someone put it, if you can't beat a giant with resources, you can beat him with ideas. CavinKare does that very well.

5

ITC-IBD

BLOWING UP THE BUSINESS MODEL

The hallmark of a truly innovative organization is that it is not afraid of completely blowing up its business model! In any industry, sooner or later, predictable pressures arise. Customers become more demanding, competition increases, commoditization occurs with the inevitable price wars, and profits get squeezed. The usual response is 'Efficiency', along with the efficiency-driving initiatives of Total Quality Management, Six Sigma, Lean Thinking and so on.

When an organization blows up its business model, it forces innovation at every level and in every area of the business. For you are compelled to blow up your processes, your methods of engagement with customers and suppliers, your products, services, hierarchies and methods of working. Each of these leads to radical innovations that can ensure an unbeatable advantage for the organization ... till this new business model is blown up again.

While efficiency is good and necessary, it can never make the earth wobble on its axis or make you an orbit shifter. When Intel was getting squeezed by competing Japanese Dynamic Random Access Memory (DRAM) chip makers, it junked its business model and exited from the memory business. Charles Schwab, the financial services firm, blew up its business model not once but twice. And it has emerged as a financial powerhouse. IBM blew up its business model, and, as Lou Gerstner, former chairman of IBM put it, the elephant danced. Closer home, the International Business Division (IBD) of the Indian conglomerate ITC Limited blew up its business model and has since emerged as one of the most influential organizations in the world.

ITC is a large Indian conglomerate with diversified businesses in packaged consumer goods, hotels, paperboard and packaging, information technology and agri business; with annual sales of US$5 billion and a market capitalization of US$18 billion. Before it blew up its business model, IBD was a small division and a small player in the mega-sized ITC world.

ITC-IBD junked its business model of food commodity trading in agricultural commodities. Although ITC was India's largest agricultural commodity player in a highly fragmented industry, it was a small insignificant player from a global perspective with single-digit market shares in most commodities it was trading in. As global markets increasingly integrated ITC was in danger of being pushed into extinction by well-heeled international agri business giants like Cargill, Mitsubishi and ConAgra to name a few. In the process of shedding its traditional business model, ITC-IBD created completely new opportunities for itself that earlier didn't exist. And it has grown: from Rs 300 crores in 1999 to about Rs 1800 crores in 2005 and Rs 3000 crores in 2008. It is now one of the most sought after trading partners in rural India. And none of this would have been possible if it hadn't decided to explode its business model.

THE CHALLENGE

It all started in 1999 when Y.C. Deveshwar, the chairman of ITC, called S. Sivakumar (the head of IBD) in to discuss IBD's future. Deveshwar made it clear that IBD needed to find ways to grow. It couldn't continue being a small Rs 300 crore company in ITC's portfolio of large businesses. Also, the risk-return ratios of this business were not considered quite favourable. They had to scale up in size to achieve economies of scale as well as to de-risk in the volatile world of agri commodity trading. Sivakumar, or Shiv as he's called, asked for resources to build infrastructure that would enable him to compete with Cargill, Mitsubishi, ConAgra and other such global commodity trading giants that owned the commodity chain end-to-end from supplier to buyer. Deveshwar said he couldn't pump in that kind of money given the low margins in the commodity trading business, but perhaps Sivakumar could try other ideas to build the business. The challenge was to create a new business model that would allow them to compete with Cargill and such others as equals, without additional investment in the kind of asset base that the global majors had. He had to think differently.

A challenge like this forces people off traditional modes of thinking and working. Mediocrity seeps into most organizations and industries because everybody is doing the 'industry standard'. What differentiates radical innovators and orbit shifters is that they *create something new* that makes a huge difference—new markets or new business models or new-to-the-world products or new-to-the-world processes. Think Steve Jobs, think Richard Branson, think Dainik Bhaskar, think Varaprasad Reddy, think Dr Venkataswamy.

As Sivakumar thought about it, he realized he needed more minds to work on cracking the challenge. And in May 1999, he called a meeting of his senior team of thirty-two people to discuss the division's options on moving forward.

But the team knew that they couldn't get new ideas with the same type of meetings or with the same kind of inputs. They had to do something different. So, rather than conduct the usual 'strategic' meeting, Shiv facilitated a going-back-to-zero visualization meet. The purpose of the meeting was to look at their business afresh—to ignore their convictions and start completely zero-based, redefining all that they took for granted. To enable this, Shiv deliberately shifted his frame of reference from that of a general manager to one of a facilitator.

The usual thinking blocks came up: they were in the commodity trading business and the only way they could grow was by following the strategies adopted by the large players in their industry; it was not possible to compete without resources; the farmers were too dispersed to organize physically, and so on. However, in this meeting they had decided beforehand to question everything that the industry took for granted—including these very beliefs. And soon, a very interesting set of ideas and realizations began to emerge.

The consistent questioning of the basics led them to make a shift: Maybe, just maybe, the existing model was not the only one for growth. Maybe e-commerce in some form could hold the key to growth. Maybe they should focus on the chain end-to-end from farmer to the final companies buying the produce whether in India or abroad. As they kept questioning the basics, they began to realize that:

(i)   They were beginning to reframe the problem in a different manner, one that had not occurred to them before;

(ii)   New, radical ideas were being generated;

(iii)   The focus of the business seemed to be shifting from commodity to servicing the unique needs of individual customers buying commodities (quality specifications, logistics, packaging, payment terms etc);

(iv)   The methodology in deciding the future strategy was shifting from a presentation to a brainstorm (that is, a far more interactive way of doing things);

(v)   The whole group seemed to be charged up about the new possibilities that existed before them.

In our experience, at typical 'strategy planning' meets, groups usually discuss the previous year's performance and use that, along with market growth statistics, to determine the next year's growth. How boring can you get? If the future is merely an extension of the past and you grow at industry-defined growth rates, why on earth would you need 'strategists' to 'plan' the way forward? Where's the magic going to come from? How are you going to put that dent in the universe?

What are your meetings like? Do your strategic meetings talk about the past? If they do they may not be strategic at all. If you're talking about maintenance, it's not strategic at all. You need to be talking instead about *destruction* and *creation*. You need to be talking about blowing up business models, processes and products; and creating new ones to take their place.

At the going-back-to-zero meets where the emerging ideas were refined over a period of three months, the team invited people from different fields and industries to share their experiences in running their businesses; they called people at the leading edge in different fields to talk to them. The team also went out to see different businesses and how they operated.

As Sivakumar and his team began to look outside their industry and began challenging everything they had till then taken for granted, something that was really strategic began to emerge.

You need two key ingredients to make *magic* happen: A 'create history aspiration' and a mindset of challenging everything that the industry takes for granted. For example, Cirque du Soleil had an aspiration to be the one show in town that every person wanted to go to. It challenged the paradigms of a circus and the theatre and the opera. And magic has happened for it. We have looked at Dainik Bhaskar and Aravind Eye Hospital. In both, the organization had a 'create history aspiration' in place and challenged everything their industry took for granted in terms of established ways of working.

ADDRESSING THE CHALLENGE: THE PROJECT SYMPHONY

Small groups began to get engaged and started working on what the possible next initiatives could be. By June 1999, the groups started discussing their ideas with one another, and by September 1999, they had come up with nearly forty propositions. Of these, four key breakthrough propositions, together called Project Symphony, were chosen:

1.   The Customer Relationship Management (CRM) initiative: Own the customer;
2.   The farmers and supply chain initiative: Choupal;
3.   The risk management initiative: Ensure;
4.   The learning initiative: Manthan.

These four initiatives were chosen because of the factors that governed the commodity trading business. The challenges that IBD faced were formidable. They were a small Indian company facing global competition—trading takes place all twenty-four hours a day across the world. And the business is highly volatile, impacted by foreign exchange fluctuations, government policies, and by the perishable nature of agricultural commodities. In this fluid, dynamic environment, you have several huge mega-corporations playing: such as Cargill, a $55 billion company; Mitsubishi, a $110 billion company; and ConAgra, a $25 billion company. Each of these had numerous offices across the globe. Against this, IBD was a puny Rs 300 crore (or $60 million) company with no offices outside the country, and with a comparatively poor supply chain infrastructure. The key question they asked themselves was: how do we deliver superior value to our customers when the existing industry leaders already have a highly efficient horizontally and vertically integrated business system? The big idea that emerged was: leverage expertise in information technology. But how was this to be done? That's how Project Symphony was born.

The first proposition under Symphony was the CRM initiative to understand the needs of customers, particularly their unique non-standard needs. This was unusual in the trading business because there are typically high levels of distrust between a buyer and a seller in this field. Buyers do not share areas of concern or weaknesses for fear that arm-twisting would take place by vendors during trading, particularly when they need the vendor's commodity the most. Also, it was felt that in the commodity business, there were unlikely to be too many unmet needs. But insight dialogues were held in thirty-five countries with eighty customers, who contributed to 70 per cent of the division's turnover. Based on the insights collated, IBD identified

The propositions for Project Symphony emerged not through a senior management brainwave, but with thirty-two minds working on the problem from different directions. Small teams went to different industries and companies to understand what they were doing and how they were doing it. Nearly thirty to forty ideas were generated that were then synthesized into four breakthrough propositions. How do breakthrough propositions happen in your organization? If the CEO alone is expected to come up with the major insights, there could be very few original ideas in the company. Ideas happen when the entire mission team is involved in generating ideas and when everyone involved steps out of the office doors to see what the rest of the world is doing.

a $1 billion opportunity space in which it could operate. The insight they got was that while everyone was operating on standard contract terms, each buyer was compromising on several unique needs—for example, quality specs, logistics, packaging etc—and the true cost of the contract was always higher than the apparent contract price! If they could find ways to plug the current gaps in terms of quality, logistics costs, assured supply, packaging etc, they would be able to provide great value addition.

That led to the second proposition: the supply chain initiative. To meet the opportunities identified above, IBD had to deliver on quality and quantity specifications, which meant that it needed better control over its supply chain, right back to the farmer. The agricultural commodity market in India is based on the village mandi system, where farmers or middlemen bring in the produce to be sold. Usually, the mandi system does not determine the quality of the product on an objective basis. Also, the produce gets aggregated, so that quality and traceability is lost due to the loss of identity of individual lots. But there was no other go, as the farmers were small and infrastructure was weak. The solution that emerged was to virtually cluster India's disparate farms, farmers and intermediaries leveraging the power of the Internet.

The third proposition was to measure and manage risk. Existing risk management tools were developed in the West which has more evolved markets with depth in trading volumes. IBD developed risk management tools specific to Indian conditions with its greater volatility caused by government interventions

Sivakumar and his team saw corporate strategy not as some ugly block of numbers and sequences of steps but as a musical symphony. We love the analogy: Strategy as Symphony, as a work of art. Strategic planning has for too long been scientific in its orientation. In discontinuous times you need a discontinuous approach. You need strategy composers who create a unique symphony, not reductionists putting together logical steps. Radical innovators see strategy not as sums adding up, but as a melding of music with one note flowing effortlessly into another. They see it as a whole. A whole that's greater than the sum of its parts. That's a key differentiator of radical innovators. None of them sees strategy as parts of a whole. None of them has worked on some parts and ignored the others. They've always worked with the whole. Each of the four propositions alone or even added together would not deliver the impact that a symphony of all the propositions would.

attempting to balance the conflicting interests of small farmers and consumers all the time.

The fourth proposition was knowledge management. The challenge was to capture and transfer tacit knowledge that resided in a few experts, converting, for example, the experience of traders into organizational knowledge that could be applied across different businesses.

As the supply chain initiative was the key to holding the symphony together, the eChoupal was conceived as a supply-chain management system, reaching right up to the primary producer—the farmer—with whom ITC had never interacted before. If quality and quantity at the producer's end could be controlled, it would lead to better servicing of ITC-IBD's customers in turn and make ITC a key differentiator in the market. ITC needed to work directly with the end producer. But it was a big challenge.

The Scale of the Challenge

To understand the scale of the challenge, one needs to understand the scale at which the food commodity business in India operates and the existing market dynamics and processes that have developed over the past few decades.

The scale is *huge*. There are hardly any large farms in India. The vast majority are small holdings of just a few hectares. There are 130 million farmers in India. To deal with the end producer in this case, unlike in other industries, means dealing with 130 million separate producers!

The costs of dealing with so many separate producers spread across the country would be astronomical. The existing intermediaries in the chain plug this gap and make up for the weak infrastructure. They actually deliver good service and make up for the inherent weaknesses in the system. On the other hand, their aggregated costs make the chain uncompetitive.

In India the farmer cannot sell directly to a private party nor can anyone buy directly from the farmer other than within the four walls of a government-regulated market yard called the mandi. The mandi system was originally created to ensure that unscrupulous buyers do not cheat the farmer. But over the years the mandi has become an intermediaries' oligopoly with the farmer now being cheated by the intermediaries instead.

The intermediaries block information flow to the farmers as they are the only interface for the farmers with the world, and because sharing market information is not in a trader's self interest. The currency that any intermediary trades in is knowledge. The farmers can only know the price at a particular mandi on a particular day by going to the mandi with the produce (though with increasing penetration of mobile phones this is changing). Once they do that, the sunken cost of transport constrains them to sell what they bring, as it becomes unviable to go to another mandi. By not letting this price information flow freely along the chain, intermediaries remove choice for the farmer, and manage to keep a large amount of the profit for themselves. The farmer makes very little, and therefore cannot invest in any sort of yield improvement practices, which in turn ensures that he lives hand to mouth.

In such an environment, it was clear that if ITC-IBD could make a difference to the farmer, it would be a huge value addition. ITC could benefit by getting the quality and quantity it desired while the farmers could benefit by getting the value they deserved as well as by having the incentive to grow higher quality crops.

But it clearly had to be a win-win proposition. There was no point replacing one exploitative system with another. If IBD went down this route, they had to ensure the farmer won as much as anyone in the system. As Shiv says, their approach is to create 'fortune at the bottom of the pyramid for their shareholders through creation of fortune for the bottom of the pyramid'.

There were some brilliant insights about how to make a difference to the farmer:

1.   Reverse the transaction. Empower the farmer rather than allow him to be at the receiving end as he has traditionally been.

2.   Unbundle what was bundled earlier. For example, information and transactions were bundled earlier. This meant that the farmer had to come to the mandi to get information about prevailing rates. With this unbundling, he would get far better choice.

3.   Bundle what was earlier unbundled. For example, to access farm management knowledge and information like weather forecasts, credit, farm inputs etc, farmers have to run from pillar to post. Instead, they could be offered a one stop shop solution at the eChoupal.

The ideas were clear and the direction was also emerging. The challenge now was to emerge with a business model that was farmer-centric and also use existing infrastructure as much as possible (the costs of changing the current method radically would be astronomical). Everything pointed to an IT model with low transaction costs that also co-opted the intermediaries. Eliminating the intermediaries totally would not only push up costs, it would also create resistance to change.

The key question the business plan had to address was: how can IBD leverage the physical transmission capabilities of these intermediaries, yet prevent them from blocking the flow of information and market signals?

The traditional answer to this would be to cut the intermediaries off and set up one's own distribution channel. But this is where the co-ownership insight came in. If they cut out the intermediaries, they would be creating a powerful force for opposition. If they co-opted them, they could work together to make this possible. The logistical support they provided was huge. If there's anything that the intermediary misused, it was information and knowledge. If these were given to the farmer, the intermediary could still make money on the volumes he handled, though his power and hold on the farmer would reduce. Thus co-opting intermediaries made business as well as social sense. The way to go was via the virtual integration of the entire value and supply chain.

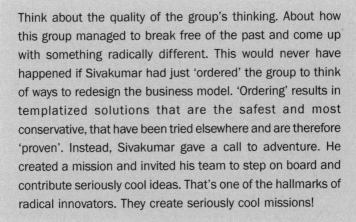

Think about the quality of the group's thinking. About how this group managed to break free of the past and come up with something radically different. This would never have happened if Sivakumar had just 'ordered' the group to think of ways to redesign the business model. 'Ordering' results in templatized solutions that are the safest and most conservative, that have been tried elsewhere and are therefore 'proven'. Instead, Sivakumar gave a call to adventure. He created a mission and invited his team to step on board and contribute seriously cool ideas. That's one of the hallmarks of radical innovators. They create seriously cool missions!

On 3 October 1999, the first physical choupal was set up to interact with the end farmer where information, knowledge and inputs were brought together on one platform. By end-October, Shiv and his team had embarked upon a feasibility study of eChoupals.

At around this time, Shiv happened to visit India Internet World and saw a Tata Consultancy Services (TCS) stall about an experimental intranet for farmers' markets in Hyderabad. This got Siva thinking in terms of the Choupal initiative and he immediately saw the scale and scope of this. And a virtual mandi fed by a network of eChoupals was born. With the business model in place, the next stage was to run a quick prototype. Around November–December 1999, the team decided to make a prototype of the eChoupal idea. They tied up with ITC Infotech to make this initiative a reality. By February 2000, the choupal website was a working model. Once they had that, they needed to get the buy-in of their top management.

ENROLLING STAKEHOLDERS

In March 2000, all business divisions of ITC had to present their business plans to the board of directors for their consideration and approval. The business plan of each division is typically about a hundred pages long, which is then summarized into four pages for circulation amongst the directors prior to the meeting of the board. The four-page document is further summarized into a one-page document on the day of the board meeting.

Shiv knew that the directors would not be able to appreciate the scope of his business plan if they read the abridged version. The synthesis of a business plan is okay for normal strategies but not for radical ones. Therefore, Siva did a one-on-one with each member before the meeting. Siva also requested the ITC chairman, Y.C. Deveshwar, at every opportunity, to read the business plan. He knew that to understand the full scope of the initiative, Deveshwar had to read the plan in its entirety. At the party prior to the presentations, Sivakumar again met Deveshwar and asked him if he had read the full text of the IBD business

plan. Deveshwar said he hadn't. Shiv insisted that he read the
full text before the presentation. In Shiv's words, 'I cornered him
and kept repeating my request till he finally gave in. The party
got over at midnight, and at 2 a.m., Deveshwar was so involved
in our strategy that he called the head of IT to read the full text
too. There is a fantastic possibility here, Deveshwar told the IT
head. The next day they changed the order of presentation,
brought eChoupal up front and continued with it for the rest of
the day.' The die was cast. ITC would back the eChoupal idea to
the hilt.

Think of the sequence of steps that Sivakumar followed to
get top management buy-in. First he created an 'articulate'
prototype. The prototype gave proof of concept. It
demonstrated that the business model was a workable
proposition. Next, before the formal presentation, he met
each board member one-on-one, explained the business
model and created individual buy-in. Only when each member
had been met one-on-one did he present the plan at the
formal meeting. Getting the main stakeholder to read the
detailed plan wasn't easy. But Shiv persisted and nagged
until he read the report.

When Deveshwar asked Siva how much he needed to make
this model see the light of day, Sivakumar said, 'Fifty lakhs.'
Deveshwar said, 'This is a great idea. Give it a full-blooded try.
Let money not be the constraint if the idea were not to work,'
and gave him Rs 10 crore! Rather than celebrate, Shiv was nervous
as it meant that he would have to earn Rs 3 crore every year as a
return on capital. But he went ahead and accepted the offer and
the challenge!

—◦❀◦—

> Sivakumar developed a complete *push* programme for getting
> supporters on board. What's your push programme like? Do
> you even have one, or are you winging it on the hope that
> someday someone will see the wisdom of your proposition?
> By all standards, Sivakumar was a relatively powerless man
> when he did this. He was the head of a small, losing division,
> a division that was under threat of closure. You don't get
> more powerless or insignificant than that. And yet he
> developed that complete push programme and saw it through.
> What's stopping you?

—◦❀◦—

Once the board's buy-in had been created, the next step was to
roll out the mission. But this was easier said than done.
Operationalizing a radical idea means overcoming radical
challenges. Teams trying to execute something breakthrough face
challenges way out of their current competency and knowledge
base and have to grow to meet the challenges and overcome them.

Operationalizing the Business Model

In each eChoupal, a locally trusted farmer was invited to become
the sanchalak or coordinator, acting as the interface between ITC
and the farming community. The computer was located in the
sanchalak's house—this was the eChoupal. Farmers from the village
and neighbouring villages came to the eChoupal and used the
sanchalak's help in accessing prices for their crops, and
understanding the real-time global rates, the price that ITC was
offering, as well as the prices prevailing at the mandis in the vicinity.

The commission agents under the mandi system, who knew
the market and farmers intimately, were incorporated as

samyojaks or collaborators. Their main roles were to identify potential sanchalaks in the villages as well as to handle logistics of procurement, storage, bagging, transportation and paperwork. For this they got a 0.5 per cent commission. They also provided high-quality information about the region's soil, expected yields, produce quality, pricing etc.

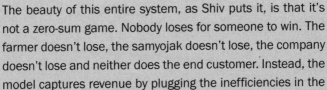

The beauty of this entire system, as Shiv puts it, is that it's not a zero-sum game. Nobody loses for someone to win. The farmer doesn't lose, the samyojak doesn't lose, the company doesn't lose and neither does the end customer. Instead, the model captures revenue by plugging the inefficiencies in the system. In any emerging economy there is latent value lying in the market that one can extract. And this is what the business model set out to do.

How does the eChoupal work? It combines a web portal in the local language and PCs with Internet access placed in the villages to create a two-way channel between ITC and the villagers. A set of websites provides the farmers with information on best practices and prevailing prices in the local and international markets. Farmers can email ITC about farming practices and also sell their products to ITC through the system.

Each eChoupal is equipped with a PC with Internet connectivity, a printer and a UPS. In case the power supply is erratic, a solar panel is provided, and if Internet connectivity is not up to the mark, a VSAT connection is provided along with another solar panel to support that.

By building a network of warehouses near the production centres and by providing inputs to the farmers and test output at the individual farm level, ITC is able to preserve the traceability of produce purchased. By helping the farmer identify and control his inputs and farming practices and by paying higher for better quality, ITC is able to improve the quality of produce that it purchases. In the commodities market, these two combine to help ITC create the differentiation that it set out to establish at the start.

The effort has paid off in the domestic markets as well. ITC is able to customize its products to local tastes, as it is able to identify the source of inputs currently. For example, the Aashirvaad brand of 'atta' that is sold in the Delhi markets has a different blend of wheat varieties, compared to the one sold in the south.

The eChoupal network is now being used to sell non-ITC products to the villages. It is also being used to provide services like rural market research to those interested. 'The next stage of the project,' says Sivakumar, 'is to provide IT-enabled services to the villages, services like health advisories, education and e-governance.' The business impact, of course, has been considerable. ITC-IBD is now a Rs 3000 crore company, and market shares have multiplied manifold. But the truly interesting part about this is that it has all largely been achieved by removing inefficiencies in the system. Nobody has to lose for everyone to win.

Thus a completely new business model was put in place that did not displace the agents of the older model but instead involved them in creating a different kind of value. This can only happen when a business is seen not as a chess game with pawns, but as a living organism. Sivakumar and his team created not so much a business model as an interdependent ecosystem. The terms frequently heard in business are 'cut-throat', 'ruthless', 'war'. Sivakumar and his team created a different way of doing business—business as an ecosystem.

Overcoming Challenges

IBD faced a host of technical challenges just going into the villages. There were bottlenecks in terms of deployment, connectivity and infrastructure. While the farmers welcomed the idea of the eChoupal, the challenge lay in actually setting it up. There were technical and manpower issues: who would host it, how would it be run, where would it be set up? The samyojaks were invaluable here in identifying lead farmers who could be sanchalaks.

But it was a technological nightmare. As there was not enough phone line penetration, they explored options such as VSAT, optic fibre connectivity, Airtel lines with group dialling, wireless in local loop, Internet through RNS or RAX Network Synchronization that enables data transmission on telephone lines, world space receivers etc. Finally, they are now setting up VSATs at every eChoupal.

Once they had resolved the connectivity problem, they found that there were electricity issues: frequent power cuts, high voltage fluctuations. The obvious solution was to use solar power packs, but, at Rs 45,000 per set, they were too expensive. However, the team kept alive its mantra of searching for a solution, and something did come up! They discovered that they did not require a permanent solar pack after all, that a battery charger at one-fourth the cost was enough—and this idea came from a farmer! All that was required was to keep the UPS running a few hours during long power outages, long enough for the data to be downloaded. So the cost reduced from Rs 45,000 to Rs 12,000. Searching for answers in a live environment helped the team find radical solutions. But the most important was the can-do attitude.

To ensure that people didn't get disheartened at the scale and number of problems that had to be overcome during deployment,

Dilution occurs at every possible opportunity. At every obstacle, every meeting with a stakeholder or a gatekeeper, dilution can occur with the scope of the project being scaled down. It's a constant battle to combat dilution, to ensure that the mission does not become a shadow of its original intent. As my colleague Rajiv Narang put it, big ideas rarely get killed; they just get diluted. Radical innovators combat dilution tooth and nail. Sivakumar knew that the eChoupal could get diluted if the regular business didn't do well. He proactively combated that dilution by setting aside a dedicated budget that would fund the mission irrespective of what happened to the regular business.

Shiv and the core leadership team created a project management culture of *rollout–fix it–scale up*. This basically said that a pioneering idea needs to be rolled out even when the solution is not perfect. There is a natural intermediate step of fixing the problems before scaling up. This approach demonstrated the tolerance for mistakes. This also developed a mindset of combating dilution, of overcoming obstacles. Ideas kept coming and were experimented with, none were rejected, and because of this, the team did not feel that any challenge was too large to take up.

Always, the impossible was overcome. Most villages had one or the other problem: no phone line or no power. But what if they did not have both? The team came up with mobile eChoupals! A Toyota Qualis was set up with a computer, large screen, battery pack etc. Again, this had to be tweaked specially to run a presentation, which was a mini-challenge in itself. It would go to the nearest eChoupal to download information, and run from village to village through the day sharing this updated information. So while the villagers did not get instant access to information, they got a status as recent as four hours old. Rollout–fix it–scale up in action.

The ITC team had anticipated people issues such as the farmers' comfort levels with using the eChoupal, their understanding of technology, etc. To address these issues, they had planned a two-day training programme for the farmers. However, they were pleasantly surprised at the outcome of the training programme—the farmers were comfortable with the whole process within half a day as against the planned two-day schedule! Additionally, there are continuous training programmes for sanchalaks to familiarize them with the Internet and with ITC's product offerings.

Internally, IBD has ensured focus for the eChoupal initiative by an over-commitment to resources. When the eChoupal took off as a new venture, they put aside a dedicated budget with the principle that, regardless of how well/poorly regular business did, this budget would not be tampered with. So the eChoupal could develop freely; it was never held to ransom by day-to-day exigencies of the business. In fact, though the trading business did not do well, eChoupal bloomed as a project.

IBD instituted a speedy decision-making process to ensure that the eChoupal did not get mired in bureaucracy. In Shiv's words, 'This was a project that was evolving, never frozen, so we did not know all the answers, which meant people needed to be free to experiment. It was better to give them a way of doing things quickly and learning from it. So we would say, if you want to try something, just go ahead, don't get caught up in filling out forms and writing requests; this can be done later. If it is a big sum/decision, pick up the phone and call the business head or the CEO anytime. No bars.'

It was a constant journey of overcoming challenges both foreseen and unforeseen. It's only when you get into operationalizing something that you encounter problems you hadn't encountered before. Here's where the prototyping mindset of rollout–fix it–learn–scale up becomes invaluable.

THE IMPACT OF THE eCHOUPAL INITIATIVE

The business impact of the eChoupal has been huge. ITC-IBD's turnover has grown from Rs 300 crore to Rs 3000 crore, profits have grown, and the aspiration is that the profits from eChoupal in seven to ten years will be more than ITC's current turnover of Rs 10,000 crore. There are currently 6500 eChoupals covering 38,000 villages and catering to more than four million farmers. The intent is to reach 100,000 villages in fifteen states over the next few years. It is also setting up rural malls called Choupal Sagars at the warehousing hubs where farmers have been bringing their produce to deliver after selling to ITC. Each Choupal Sagar is intended to serve all the needs of a farming community— retailing everything from tractors to toothpastes, everything that earlier a farmer had to travel to town to buy. It also provides facilities like a medical centre, a crop advisory centre, a soil testing centre and so on. There are twenty-four Choupal Sagars already up and running.

Through the eChoupal, IBD has changed the business model of commodity trading. By marrying technology with trading in rural markets, IBD has brought in a new paradigm. The strategy of dealing with the end farmer directly has been very successful with both farmers and the erstwhile middlemen being co-opted.

Before the eChoupal initiative, IBD was 'just another non-core' activity within the ITC Group and it was on the verge of being divested. Today, however, IBD is one of the core businesses of ITC and has created a multi-category distribution highway for the ITC Group in rural India. It is reaching rural India like never before and is becoming a channel partner for other firms too. IBD also forms an integral part of the packaged branded food business launched by ITC recently.

The success of the eChoupal initiative has also helped ITC acquire a position of influence on e-commerce matters in the country. Both Shiv and Deveshwar are regular speakers on e-governance, rural development, etc., and IBD has become a globally known company. Further, Shiv has been invited to talk at World Bank forums, as well as at the World Earth Summit in Johannesburg. He has also advised the Planning Commission on how e-commerce can be used in emerging economies to deliver value for farmers. The expertise on e-commerce matters that currently resides within the ITC Group as a result of the eChoupal project has been converted into a 'consulting business proposition' by ITC Infotech.

A business division on the verge of closure has emerged as one of the most powerful growth engines in the ITC group. Today, it's an international case study, and its competitors—among the most powerful names in international commodities trading—have been sidelined. Its head advises the Government of India on rural issues, and he is a much sought after advisor on rural transformation across the globe with governments calling on him to advise them. *None of this would have been possible if IBD hadn't blown up its business model. Is the IBD story telling you something explosive?*

6

BOSCH INDIA

INNOVATION BLOWBACK INTO EUROPE

Some of the biggest breakthroughs are breathtakingly simple and they come from a complete reframing of a problem or challenge. In 1993, Apple, under its CEO John Sculley, tried creating a Personal Digital Assistant or PDA called 'Newton' that could recognize human handwriting as an input device rather than use a keyboard. It failed miserably at the handwriting recognition. The technology was just not up to it. They had spent nearly $500 million trying to develop it and had failed. Other companies, too, tried to develop a similar handheld device that could recognize handwriting. Nearly a billion dollars spent overall in this endeavour went down the drain. Palm Computing was one of the other companies that failed. But then Jeff Hawkins, the CEO of Palm Computing, reflected on his failure and thought about reframing the challenge. Rather than develop complex software that could enable a machine to recognize all kinds of handwriting styles, why not teach people to write in a way that the machine could understand? He created Graffitti—a kind of writing that requires users to make modified characters with a single pen stroke. It's easy to learn and easy for the machine to recognize. The result was the now iconic Palm Pilot which was launched in 1997. It was developed at a cost of $3 million and by 2000 was generating revenues of over a billion dollars a year. And all because of a reframe!

Closer home, a team from Bosch India, the Indian wing of the global engineering giant, the Bosch Group, broke industry norms through a similar reframe in a different context. Stringent emission norms for diesel engines currently require extensive engine modifications to enable them to interact with a complex external high-pressure pump that aids in reducing emissions. The team from Bosch India reframed this challenge: Rather than make major and expensive engine modifications to enable it to interact with the high-pressure pump, why not make modifications to the pump to enable it to interact with the existing engine and give the same results?

Like all great truths, it seems self-evident today but at the time, the challenge of creating a pump that could enable an existing traditional engine to meet the rigorous emission norms without modifications was seen as so far off the wall as to be almost impossible. No one thought in these terms. They only thought about how and when to convince engine manufacturers to modify their traditional diesel engines. With stricter emission norms coming in, it only seemed a matter of time. But the team at Bosch India began flirting with the idea of creating a pump— since it is the pump or the fuel injection system that has the greatest impact on emission.

The key challenge was that it was considered impossible to do this with the existing engines. Expensive and extensive modifications would need to be made to the engines. Could the team think radically and find an alternate way of doing this?

They did, and now, existing diesel engines can move to the

stringent emission norms of Euro IV, V, and VI without expensive engine modifications that would cost anywhere from Euros (€) 3 million to €20 million. All it needs is a 20-Euro pump called the PF-45 that can be modified to fit any existing diesel engine. And the impact has been tremendous. It was launched in 2006 with expected sales of 70,000 units in 2007. Instead, 160,000 units were sold according to company sales figures. And in 2010, one million units are expected to be sold! The impact on the industry is that many engines can continue with the existing design right up to Euro VI—the highest emission norms currently envisaged.

THE CHALLENGE: THE BEGINNING

It all began in 1989–90. Bosch India had been made the centre of competence for a particular single-cylinder pump called the PF pump used in diesel engines. By 2002, the realization had set in for the R&D group that PF pumps would soon become extinct as the world was moving to tighter emission norms which required a different type of fuel injection system called the common rail system. PF pumps catered to the older kind of engines that could only meet Euro II emission norms at best. To go beyond would need a high-pressure pump for the common rail system.

Moving to Euro IV and higher norms would necessitate all older diesel engines shifting to common rail systems and making extensive modifications to existing diesel engines. The modifications would need to be in both the drive and the crank-case, the most expensive part of the engine. These modifications, especially in developed economies, could cost anything up to €20 million for the manufacturer, depending on the kind and size of engine. This would also mean the end of the PF pump.

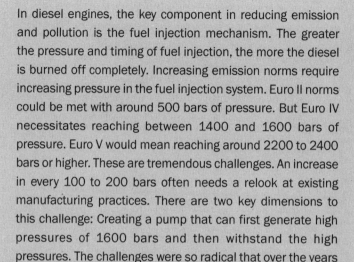

In diesel engines, the key component in reducing emission and pollution is the fuel injection mechanism. The greater the pressure and timing of fuel injection, the more the diesel is burned off completely. Increasing emission norms require increasing pressure in the fuel injection system. Euro II norms could be met with around 500 bars of pressure. But Euro IV necessitates reaching between 1400 and 1600 bars of pressure. Euro V would mean reaching around 2200 to 2400 bars or higher. These are tremendous challenges. An increase in every 100 to 200 bars often needs a relook at existing manufacturing practices. There are two key dimensions to this challenge: Creating a pump that can first generate high pressures of 1600 bars and then withstand the high pressures. The challenges were so radical that over the years a different kind of pump itself has been developed—the Common Rail pump. The pump is large, has three pumping chambers (pressuring units), a metering unit and a drive.

Fundamentally, it was a question of survival for the team and production unit.

Internally, there was also the feeling that Common Rail (CR) is the present and PF is the past. The CR team in India looked at the PF team as a relic from the past. Even the organization was focused towards CR, while PF was just about tolerated. There were also questions about the contribution of the product development team internally. After all, they were just modifying and tweaking Bosch Germany's products. What was their contribution at all?

The R&D team of the PF pump group in India, headed by R. Baskaran, deputy general manager, product engineering, decided to do something about this. If they could find ways to make the

PF pump as effective as the conventional Common Rail pump, perhaps extensive engine block modifications would not be required. And engine manufacturers could use existing engines but with higher emission norm capability, thus saving millions of dollars in development costs. This was especially true for India, where we're currently on Euro III equivalent emission norms. Once India moves to Euro IV for commercial vehicles, extensive engine modifications would need to take place, perhaps leading to increased vehicle costs.

To give an analogy about the scope of the challenge: Look at propeller and jet planes. In the first half of the 20th century, propeller aircraft kept improving and getting better and better. They began to fly higher, farther and faster. But there was always a limit they could not go beyond in terms of speed, distance and height. It needed a jet engine to do this. Similarly, in terms of pressure, there was always a limit the PF pump couldn't go beyond. It needed a Common Rail pump to reach there. What the PF pump team at Bosch India was trying to do in a way was to make the propeller plane perform at the same levels as a jet plane, without the additional costs that a jet plane would entail.

THE ROAD FROM IDEA TO IMPLEMENTATION

In principle, the PF group had an idea that they could create such a pump. But they would need a customer willing to go along with the idea and give it a try. This would also allow Bosch to put in the resources required to develop such a pump. They found a customer not in India but in Germany: the Deutz group that manufactures diesel engines for customers like Volvo and Renault.

Deutz was entering a new product category and didn't have a history of using Common Rail systems. The trigger was an order that they got from Volvo for medium-duty trucks. They decided to give this a try. As Dr Thiemann of Deutz says, they didn't want to make extensive design modifications to the existing engine. And when they decided to go with Bosch to co-develop this new pump, there were a lot of concerns within Deutz. First, Common Rail systems were new to the company and they had no experience in this. Second, they were trying to create an 'exotic' system that was unique. Would it work at all? Were they just wasting time and money?

The Bosch team from both Germany and India managed to convince Deutz that they would be able to develop such an 'exotic' system. The R&D, of course, would happen in India as the centre of competence for PF pumps was based here. Deutz decided to go ahead and commit to the development and also share developmental costs. A development timetable and budget

---

What's fascinating about this team is that they didn't shrug their shoulders and say that it's inevitable that the world moves from PF to CR as emission norms tighten. They didn't wait for events to overtake them and instead decided to take control and do something within their sphere of influence. And by the way, how much of a sphere of influence do you think a small group in a category going out of fashion would have? They may not have realized at the time, but they had the influence to impact the entire diesel industry across the world. How much of an influence do most of us think we have? Many of us feel fairly helpless and limited in our ability to make an impact. In reality, we may have far more influence and ability to impact the world than we realize.

---

was chalked out. The pump would need to be developed by 2005. It was 2002.

While the developmental timetable had been chalked out, there were organizational, human and technical challenges that the team faced. One organizational challenge was that internally across Bosch there was a great degree of scepticism and also resistance to the idea of a new pump. And as Dr Gerhard Ziegler, the VP of engineering application, says, the project had to be kept under the radar in the beginning. If it had been very visible, it could have run into internal hurdles. Once the team demonstrated that the pump was viable and actually emerged with one, it was brought out into public view and the accolades followed, as this was the first time at Bosch that a new-to-the world product had been developed in India.

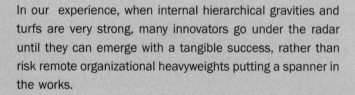

In our experience, when internal hierarchical gravities and turfs are very strong, many innovators go under the radar until they can emerge with a tangible success, rather than risk remote organizational heavyweights putting a spanner in the works.

The human challenges were around belief in capability. If you think about it, product innovation often flows from the developed world into India. It rarely flows the other way. The belief we have managed to create for ourselves is that we are good at replication and 're-engineering'. We take anything developed anywhere in the world and create a damned good version of that within a few weeks. For years, we have actually been taking pride in this. But create something new to the world, especially something highly engineered? Forget about it. We don't have the capability. We don't believe we have the capability, and by extension, we create the perception internationally too that we don't have the capability.

It is no different at MNCs in India. Indian arms of MNCs are often seen as minor operations that tinker around at the margins. In many cases the Indian arm just makes modifications to products developed in the West. Too often in the Indian arm of an MNC, R&D is a misnomer. More tweak and modify takes place than true research and development. The 'R&D' department just tinkers with an existing product to 'adapt' it to 'Indian conditions'.

This was true of Bosch India as well. A team member says that he was very afraid when he took up the project. Earlier he had worked only on the mechanical pumps and there too just tweaking existing products. Here, for the first time, he was expected to develop from scratch. There was a great sense of fear about whether he would be able to do so. Adding to his anxiety was the knowledge that this was a very important project for Bosch India.

The technical challenges were also tremendous. The key constraint was that it would have to be a single-cylinder pump that fitted into the existing engine block and created no changes or modifications in the existing engine. In shape, it would have to look a lot like the existing PF pumps, but in performance it would have to deliver in terms of a conventional Common Rail pump.

The key challenge is to deliver the required fuel quantity at 1600 bar pressure with the single-cylinder PF pump. This was possible with the three pumping units in case of the conventional Common Rail (CR) pump, but considered impossible with the single-cylinder pump. The maximum a single-cylinder pump could reach was pressures of around 750 bars. To reach Euro IV norms, the pump would need to withstand a pressure of at least 1600 bars.

THE INNOVATIONS

Now the innovations began. The team was working in a sphere of uncertainty. They didn't know whether this was even possible. To begin with, they decided to challenge every part of the existing Common Rail pump. The conventional CR pump has three key components: a driving unit, three pumping units, and a built-in fuel quantity regulating unit. The key reframe the team attempted here was to 'unbundle' the 'bundled'. They separated the bundled components and decided to challenge each component, beginning with the driving unit. They challenged the fact that the pump required an external drive. Why couldn't it be attached to the engine cam shaft and use that to drive the pump and generate pressure? They did away with the drive unit and the pump is now inside the engine block.

The next challenge was to do away with the three sections of the conventional CR pump. The three sections aided in generating pressure. They did this by using the cam lobe in the shape of a triangle that really gave a 3-time lift so that as the engine camshaft drove the pump, one revolution in effect lifted and dropped the plunger 3 times. This created the same effect as the 3 sections of a conventional CR pump.

Some challenges that seemed very minor took up a huge time and effort. For instance, during trials they found

> The shift they made here was to utilize unutilized assets like the engine cam shaft. If you think about it, what are some unutilized assets in your organization? There are often tremendous assets lying around unutilized which often need just a reframe to utilize them in completely new ways.

that there were huge stresses on the guide pin at the cam. It took them nearly a year just to find a way to deal with those immense stresses and then to test it. Testing meant making the section go through 10^7 trials—ten million trials. And that took time and effort. The pump had to work perfectly. One challenge they had committed to was that it would last for 500,000 hours of usage— up from the existing 150,000 hours for the conventional CR pump. So nothing could be allowed to go wrong there. Five hundred thousand hours really means a lifespan of twenty years.

The fuel quantity regulating unit of the conventional CR pump was separated and placed elsewhere so that it didn't take up precious space in the engine block.

The next challenge was to create an external body that could withstand tremendous pressures and temperatures. This was done using a monoblock, but then the team found that the plunger seized because the temperature was so high that the body became deformed. They needed to work on this further. One solution was to coat the interior with anti-friction and anti-wear carbon-impregnated coating.

Finally, the radical pump was created. It was developed within budget and within time. Deutz got the pump in the time frame they had wanted it. It collected a patent along the way and took constant innovations at every level and in every part of the pump as each new challenge required an innovation to crack it.

The biggest constraints to a product are those that enable it to succeed. For instance, the biggest enabler to propeller planes was the propeller. And until that was removed, the jet didn't happen. Similarly, the biggest enabler to the usual CR pump were the external drive and the three pressure chambers. Once these were removed, the innovative PF-45 pump happened.

What are some key enablers of *your* product that you can eliminate?

THE IMPACT

The impact has been tremendous. Business has boomed. And since the pump is now so incredibly simple, the assembly, installation and maintenance costs have crashed. A large part of servicing costs in Common Rail pumps has always been pump servicing by highly trained technicians. This has been all but eliminated. The pump needs no servicing and lasts more than three times as long as a conventional CR. And at around 20 Euros, at a fourth the cost of a conventional CR pump, it's really great value for money.

The impact on Bosch India has been incredible. There has always

Really, if you think about it, talent is like capital. It flows to the place of highest utilization. At Bosch India, every year, around thirty new engineering graduates join and they get to choose which department they want to join. Usually, only about five or six join R&D. But last year, twenty-four out of thirty graduates wanted to join R&D! Once the R&D team began producing breakthrough innovations, it began attracting talent. A similar story is found at Titan after it created the world's slimmest water resistant watch and at Tata Motors after the Nano challenge. A new kind of talent is seeking out these companies. The newspapers are full of the 'reverse brain-drain' or 'brain-gain' with Indians who had migrated to the US coming back home. This really is a manifestation of talent going to the place of highest utilization. So really, if you are not satisfied with your in-house talent, the catch is that you are not going to attract new talent without demonstrating fundamental breakthroughs with your existing talent. And these breakthroughs will largely come from an orbit-shifting challenge like the one the Bosch team took up.

been a fear that manufacturing and development could shift to China to take advantage of costs. With nothing to differentiate between India and China, the fear was that this would just be a matter of time. Today, with the innovations that India is producing around the pump, this fear has, for the time being at least, reduced.

The potential impact on the diesel engine industry is huge. Engine manufacturers and commercial vehicle buyers have got a new lease of life as they don't have to go in for expensive engine modifications to meet the next level of emission norms. Instead, they can get the same benefit for a fraction of the cost. This pump can also be upgradable to meet Euro VI norms that will come into force in 2013 in Europe and 2020 in India (India lags behind Euro norms by around eight years).

The impact on the internal team has been awesome. The India competency centre has suddenly become extremely visible not only to the Bosch world, but to the entire diesel world. The R&D department is attracting talent. Last year, 80 per cent of new engineering trainees at Bosch India wanted to join R&D, up from 20 per cent in previous years.

Internal motivation and confidence have skyrocketed. As a team member said, 'I feel like a boy who's won a gold medal.' Another said, 'I now feel confident about taking on any challenge. The PF-45 experience has really motivated us and boosted our confidence.' There is a deep sense of pride. As a team member said, 'We have always felt that we Indians cannot do any development. Everything can only be developed in Europe and brought to India a decade later when the world has shifted to other products and technologies. We get the hand-me-

The usual block to innovation in a developing country like India is the question: 'Has anyone done it before? If no one has done it before how can we do it?' This often leads to 'fitting-in' and modifying rather than creating new-to-the-world innovations.

downs to lead. Today we have shown the world that we can conceive, develop and manufacture terrific innovations.' The mindset shift has been from 'we are just applicators for Bosch Germany's products, therefore make minimal tweaks after extensive permission-seeking' to 'we create technology that nobody in the world has done. We are thought leaders'. The team has overcome the traditional developing country mindset of deference to the West or Japan.

The same team has now developed the next-generation pump called PF-51 which is a much smaller version of the current one. As Amarnath from sample manufacturing said, the pump is the epitome of simplicity and performance. It does what a PF-45 does at one-fourth its dimensions and weight. And the fascinating factor, according to the project champion Baskaran, is that now, new engine manufacturers are designing their engines around the pump rather than the usual pump manufacturers designing the pump around the engine. This next-generation pump has created tremendous breakthroughs in design, cost reduction and size.

But perhaps the greatest impact is the 'innovation blowback' effect. A pump originally conceived for India, keeping in mind the reluctance of most Indian commercial vehicle customers to spend anything extra on vehicle costs, is now sweeping the European continent. What began as an idea to make a painless transition to higher emission norms in India has now impacted the Western hemisphere. Increasingly, innovations from India, developed to meet the uniquely Indian challenges of extreme low-cost solutions along with great quality are impacting the West. The PF-45 pump is one such innovation.

And it all began when one 'powerless' team decided to take control of its own destiny and began by reframing something the whole diesel world had begun to take for granted.

SECTION III

ENROLLING TO A CAUSE

If you want to build a ship, don't drum up the men to gather wood, divide the work and give orders. Instead, teach them to yearn for the vast and endless sea.

—Antoine de Saint-Exupery

Enrolling is not about getting people to sign on. It's about reaching people at a fundamental level and making them bigger champions of the mission than you. When Sivakumar of ITC-IBD enrolled his chairman, Y.C. Deveshwar, the story goes that Deveshwar became so passionate about the idea that he took over Sivakumar's presentation to the board and began doing it himself.

Enrolment is about demonstrating complete ownership. It doesn't happen through numbers or targets. It happens through a cause. And every single orbit shifter in this book was able to create that cause.

Enrolment needs an operating principle of thinking win-win-win. As Ranjan Malik puts it, he goes in with the operating principle of three entities winning: the context has to win, he has to win and the others involved have to win. When ITC-IBD went out to enrol people they may have followed a similar operating principle. The context (eChoupal and the farmer) won, they won, and others involved won by becoming Sanchalaks or Samyojaks.

Rajiv Narang also advocates the operating principle of 'Enrol through Cause and Resonance, never Exploitation'. As he says, 'If you think you are exploiting the other person, you are always on the back foot. Always raise the thinking to the level of the cause and then self-enrolment happens.' Rajiv tends to enrol not at the level of self-actualization, but at the level of self-transcendence by inviting people to join in a larger cause. To take a case in point, an organization wanted to work only with A-category management institutes and negotiations had got bogged down on that score. Rajiv spoke to the head of that organization about the larger purpose: to develop the B- and C-category management institutes. Everybody wants to be associated with the A-category ones, but the transformation of the country would happen only if the B- and C-category institutes also developed. And that is the larger purpose. The organization immediately signed on. Most people *want* to contribute towards making a real difference.

Varaprasad Reddy also enrolled through self-transcendence when he enrolled people from across countries and cultures to his cause of eliminating Hepatitis B. To the extent that the wife of one of the scientists who was helping him out from the US began complaining about the phone bills the scientist was running up. Most of Shantha Biotech's employees joined because of the cause.

Another key operating principle in enrolment is to move from an unconditional 'no' to a conditional 'yes'. Most people don't object to an entire idea or proposal. They object to certain parts of it. Movement happens when you get them to articulate what it would take to move from an unconditional 'no' to a conditional 'yes'. The M.V. Foundation works to release children from bonded labour and put them into full-time schools. They enrol multiple stakeholders from the landlord to the parents to the child, the larger community, teachers, to government officials. Many of these have conflicting priorities. And yet through patiently moving each person and each entity from unconditional no-s to conditional yes-es, MVF's volunteers have managed to put more than twelve lakh children into full-time school.

Enrolling is not selling. And perhaps the key difference is that in enrolling you are asking the person to *contribute*. In selling you are trying to sell benefits to him. You are trying to 'give' him something. But in enrolling, you are exciting him enough to take independent action for your mission. Perhaps even give up something.

In the biographies of the orbit-shifting missions that follow, Trichy Police and Chola Vehicle Finance enrolled their team members at a fundamental level, leading to immense passion and energy, and consequently completely turned around their respective organizations.

7

TRICHY POLICE

SHIFTING POLICING PARADIGMS

India as a country is globally the most affected by terrorism. Terrorists strike with impunity in city after city. The deaths in India far outnumber those of any other country. And every time a terrorist attack occurs there is much hand wringing and statements by police and politicians that they will do more. For this they need more cops, more intelligence, more equipment, and more and harsher laws.

But there are pockets of excellence that exist in the country where crime and terror have been contained. The Trichy police has dealt with and contained terrorism and it's not happened with more equipment, cops or laws. Instead, in true breakthrough innovation fashion, it's happened with *less*—less policing, less equipment, and fewer or the same laws.

To give a sense of the scale of impact, how many cops do you think it takes to keep peace in a city of twenty-four lakhs; and not just keep peace, but reduce crime as well as nip budding terrorism, and do this in a city polarized by religion? In the global experience of policing, the number of cops required for this kind of population is around 7000. The more developed countries in Europe average around 5000 cops for a population this size. The police force in Trichy, Tamil Nadu, did it with only 260 constables! Trichy police brought down crime by 40 per cent, nipped extremism and terrorism in the bud and they did it with 260 constables out of a total force of 2600 policemen in the entire force. And these 260 weren't crack, highly trained commandos and assault troops but ordinary constables of the kind we encounter on the streets of India every day. How did this happen, and what lessons can the rest of the country learn from Trichy?

The Beginning

It all began in 1999. Trichy, an unusual mix of communities— one-third Hindu, one-third Muslim and one-third Christian— was an emerging hotbed of fundamentalism then. A community leader had been killed and the city was tense. Explosives had been planted in Police establishments. Alienation between communities was growing. The police was barely tolerated and cops lived in fear after attacks on them. A particular police officer was targeted for his bold action against Muslim fundamentalists at Coimbatore. Grenades had been hurled at him in an attempt by the fundamentalists to take revenge and to deter the police from taking any further action against them. Communal tensions were rising following the Coimbatore bomb blasts and in this cauldron, A.B. Vajpayee, the then prime minister, L.K. Advani, the then home minister and a host of Bharatiya Janata Party (BJP) leaders were expected to arrive. The possibility of such high security-risk figures arriving in their midst was giving sleepless nights to the police force in charge of security and overall peace in the city. There were fears of a possible terror attack on the BJP conference being held there. At this stage, a new man took over as commissioner of police in Trichy: J.K. Tripathy, an IPS officer of the 1985 batch.

Stop for a moment, and ask yourself: if you were in Tripathy's shoes what would you have done? In our experience, most people, when reaching a point of diminishing returns, try 'harder'. They try doing more of the same. They would have pushed their intelligence wing harder to get more information, made demands on them that they were in no position to deliver because the world had shifted. The blasts had brought polarization and suspicion and as a result, intelligence was drying up. Doing more of the same when the world has shifted doesn't work.

THE MAN, THE MISSION

Within two years of Tripathy's taking over, Trichy had been transformed. As many as 261 dreaded criminals were nabbed and the crime rate dropped by about 40 per cent, an eventuality until then considered impossible. For, it was thought that crime could only increase, or at best be contained, but that it could not drop. Today, a decade later, Trichy is a city at peace and a lighthouse of communal amity. Public–police relationships are at a scale unprecedented for India. Policemen are called 'anna' not out of fear but out of respect and regard. They get invited to functions and marriages. All the stakeholders—community, police, politicians, bureaucrats and NGOs—work together in considerable harmony. And more importantly, for a city seething with communal anger prior to 1999, there have been no incidents of communal violence since. The police have become an integral part of the community, and this isn't some 'advanced' Western country we are talking of. It has happened right here in India, in less than two years and has been sustained for a decade.

How did the transformation happen?

The first problem that Tripathy faced was that there was no intelligence. And how does one prevent a possible terror attack without intelligence? There are two major kinds of intelligence: human intelligence and non-human intelligence. Non-human intelligence includes all forms of wire tapping, phone tapping, electronic eavesdropping and so on. Human intelligence is of two kinds: police informer-based and spontaneous community intelligence where the local community and neighbourhood share information with the police regularly. In Trichy, police informer intelligence was no great shakes, and all sources of community intelligence had dried up because alienation of the police force from the community was near complete. The police were seen as thugs and crooks who bullied the poor and the weak and fawned upon the powerful—a reflection of public–police relationships anywhere in India. For instance, when you think of the police in your city, what images and associations come to mind? Not very flattering, I am sure. And this is precisely the perception of cops that Tripathy faced, only several magnitudes higher.

The first challenge for Tripathy was to actually get intelligence in. With the BJP leaders' visit only a month away, there was precious little time to set up an intelligence infrastructure. So Tripathy had to think out of the box and do something radical. He selected fifty of his most reliable men—constables who had a 'good' record. 'Good' meant honest: they were not known to take bribes, had no bad habits like drinking or womanizing, and were polite to others, especially the public. They were asked to stay in their home localities for a week and their only job was to observe what was happening and listen and pass on to Tripathi information related to security threats. They didn't have to physically report at their police stations. He gave them his mobile number and they were to call him at any time of the day or night with information.

The quality of information that Tripathy received was stupendous, and it enabled him to take preventive actions that ensured that the prime minister's visit and the BJP convention went off smoothly.

As Tripathy puts it, we do need to spend money in acquiring the latest technology and equipment. But this will not help unless community sharing of knowledge and support exists. As he says, most terrorists and criminals cannot get a foothold without local support. Local support is *always* essential for any crime. Terrorists and criminals are great at exploiting and magnifying any neighbourhood and community hurts, any grievances, and using these to their advantage by taking an extreme position and garnering support by providing a promise of revenge or aid. They get the disgruntled on their side and unfortunately, even those who are not part of their extreme credo keep quiet and don't inform the cops because they don't know whom to inform and because they don't trust the cops.

THE COMMUNITY POLICING MODEL

Once the immediate security issue had been addressed and dealt with, Tripathy decided to extend this method to intelligence on crime. The constables told him that their rapport with their neighbours was increasing and that they were able to renew old contacts.

Tripathy now hit upon the idea of experimenting with the community policing model that has worked so well in developed democracies. He told the constables to continue to stay in their localities and feed him information—this time on crime. Again, the results were excellent. He also found, however, that this time there was resistance from the station house officers (SHOs), mainly because this ate into their corruption. Earlier, they could always deny knowledge of a crime or awareness of a criminal's location. But with the pinpointed information that was flowing in, lack of knowledge/awareness could no longer be forwarded as an excuse and they had to act on the information.

Resistance from the SHOs could take various forms: they could plead lack of strength, say that manpower was getting diverted and affecting routine operations, indulge in sabotage by sending in poor quality personnel to make important arrests, or any of the other methods of passive-aggression. Tripathy overcame this by making himself the recipient of information. The constables informed him and he, in turn, informed the

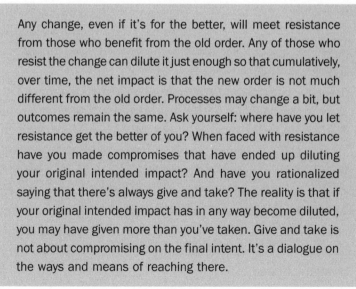

Any change, even if it's for the better, will meet resistance from those who benefit from the old order. Any of those who resist the change can dilute it just enough so that cumulatively, over time, the net impact is that the new order is not much different from the old order. Processes may change a bit, but outcomes remain the same. Ask yourself: where have you let resistance get the better of you? When faced with resistance have you made compromises that have ended up diluting your original intended impact? And have you rationalized saying that there's always give and take? The reality is that if your original intended impact has in any way become diluted, you may have given more than you've taken. Give and take is not about compromising on the final intent. It's a dialogue on the ways and means of reaching there.

SHOs. Soon, results started coming in and crime dropped dramatically in these localities.

After a month, when Tripathy thought he had experimented enough, he decided to scale up a modified version of the experiment across Trichy. He now had a workable model to deal with a question that had plagued him since his police academy days: 'Why are the police so ineffective given the fact that on an average only 3 per cent of the population engages in criminal activities?' The answer: because they lack public support. The police force today continues the legacy of colonial rule, when it was a force for suppression. The rulers have changed, but the ground reality hasn't. The state still uses the force as a tool of repression. The police currently draw their power through the Constitution and not through the support of the people. If they could get this support, the police force would become much more trusted and, therefore, more effective.

> Radical innovators like Tripathy are often extremely dissatisfied with the status quo. They see a world that everyone else takes for granted and ask: 'Why can't it be different?' The number one reason more people aren't radical innovators is because they fail to imagine a different world.

Tripathy worked fast because he wasn't sure how much time he had. In almost all his postings, he had been transferred within five to six months because he refused to cooperate with the powers that be in anything smacking of corruption. If he had to make a difference, he had to move very fast. Once he decided to scale up, he did some thinking and realized that intelligence and support from the community cannot come just by asking for it. To build a sustainable model, there need to be shifts at a mindset level in the community and in the entire social ecosystem at large.

There were three key shifts required:

1. To shift the police mindset from dealing with crime and criminals to actively serving a community: to shift from the police seeing themselves as enforcers who are distinct from the community to actually being a part of the community. This would then enable the community

> Rather than debate too long on making the perfect plan, radical innovators recognize that the perfect plan just doesn't exist. Instead, they go ahead with an idea, prototype it, mature it through ongoing live experiments and then roll it out.

to see them as true 'rakhwalas' (protectors). There also had to be a shift from reacting to crime and responding once a complaint or FIR is launched, to actively preventing crime by seeking out the potential crime triggers and neutralizing them before they became active.

2. To shift communities from anonymity and fragmentation to familiarity and cohesion. Most crime happens because of the anonymity that exists in cities and neighbourhoods. Neighbourhood communities are often fragmented on religious, professional and economic lines. A shift was required to build cohesion and ownership of the neighbourhood across *all* sections of society in that neighbourhood.

3. To move from a silo-based 'department first' approach of all government departments to a holistic 'purpose first' problem-solving approach across departments.

Shifting the Police Mindset and the Police–Public Dynamic

Tripathy's first step was to shift the police mindset and reframe the police–public relationship. He began by choosing the right policemen. He screened the 2600-odd police force and handpicked 260 constables on the basis of internal police personal files, followed by verifications. He picked those with no record of corruption, no bad habits, and with a track record of effectiveness. They were rigorously screened by Tripathy personally. He met each person a number of times and short-listed 260 who seemed most open to change. This was done in one week! The screening was done for two reasons: one, to select the best constables and, two, to decide which environment they would best fit into. Thus, those who were more educated and comparatively gentler would fit into an area where the socio-economic profile was higher, while those who were comparatively 'tougher' would fit into, say, a slum environment. This fitting of

---

In any mission or cause, one of the first things that orbit shifters do is to get the best—the most passionate lead radicals and influencers—on board. These lead radicals are those who are happy to go where no man has gone before. They are the rebels, the ones dissatisfied with the status quo, the ones thirsting for a change. And all they need is a mission, a cause ... and an orbit shifter to ignite them. How does it work in your organization? Unfortunately, in our experience with organizations, extraordinary ideas are often pursued in spare time by people who can be spared. The best people look after immediate priorities, while growth missions that determine the organization's future and that require the best people are often pursued by people who can be spared—and these are never the stars of the organization. Is your tomorrow in the hands of those not competent enough to handle your today?

the person to the environment was an important part of the selection process.

Once Tripathy had short-listed the best people, he created ownership and buy-in by bringing about an awareness of the non-personality factors that lead to crime. He would ask them about their early years and their childhood friends and what they were doing now. It turned out that quite a few were not doing much. So he asked, 'You have come from such and such place ... why aren't there more like you there? What opportunities/breaks did you get that they didn't?'

This dialogue created a higher awareness that people weren't born criminals, that it was the environment that played a major role in antisocial and criminal activities. People often take to crime because it's the easiest way out. When they grow up in severely deprived localities and they see that the rule of law is neither fair nor equitable, they take to crime to earn a living. If we could improve the environment, we could limit antisocial activity.

The next challenge was to build ownership. After Tripathy got the right people in and identified who would go where, he started his project without any delay. Everything was co-evolved with the constables. He suggested a beat system of four people to a beat, who wouldn't be moved for at least two years, and asked them how this could be made to work. Whatever suggestions the constables gave were immediately experimented with. As he says, 'If I had started with a lecture on community policing, it would not have penetrated except at an intellectual level. They began without knowing the principle. They just did it. They learnt on the job, saw results, came back and asked for more information. When they asked for more information, I got community-policing articles translated into Tamil for them. They read the notes and came back saying, "This is similar, but ours is unique because *we*

Tripathy constantly strove to create ownership. He began by asking for suggestions on how the beat system could be implemented. When people give ideas, they begin the process of getting involved. Seeking ideas is one of the first steps to increasing involvement. When a person gives you an idea, he gives you a part of himself. And when he gives you a part of himself, his involvement has already increased. The next step to creating ownership is to sit at a table and have a common thrashing out of on-field problems. When a group sits together at a table and works out ways to overcome problems, the resultant shared ownership that emerges is tremendous. But possibly the greatest contributor to ownership is end-to-end holistic responsibility. When people have total control and end-to-end responsibility over their areas, they tend to have the greatest possible emotional involvement.

have developed it rather than the bosses"'. This one factor created tremendous ownership.

Another factor that led to ownership was Tripathy ensuring that he involved the constables in decision making. He asked them, 'Tell me what problems will we/do we face, and how should we go about overcoming them?' The constables were initially not very aware of the possibilities, so he needed to bring in additional information like government policies and schemes where people had benefited. From that kind of information, ideas started flowing. And because ideas came from the individuals themselves, it led to tremendous ownership. As Tripathy says, 'It's very easy to issue orders. But that way only I am the owner. And when the next person comes in, he changes things with his own orders. Institutionalization happens when people below take up issues and solve them.'

The community policing model that Tripathy followed was similar to the one followed by developed countries, but not the same. Given Indian conditions, the police had to play a much more proactive role in the community, especially in civic and corporation/municipality issues. The constables were called 'beat officers' and groups of four were made responsible for a locality. Sixty localities or 'beats' were created. The beat officers had the following 'benefits' or status rewards: 1) They didn't have to report to the police station for roll call every morning, like the other constables did; 2) They were given walkie-talkies—only officers use them normally. Out of four persons in a beat, one

The one thing that differentiates NGOs and other social organizations from business ones is that social organizations tend to have a dedicated pool of emotionally involved leaders who are developed through handling end-to-end projects and responsibilities. Business organizations on the other hand tend to have compartmentalized functions. While these may have contributed to efficiency in an earlier, more stable era, in today's turbulent times when entrepreneurship is a key requirement, these compartments stifle entrepreneurship. How can an organization develop entrepreneurship in a business head when purchasing is out of his control, when a common sales force handles both his business' products as well as those of other businesses within the group? What kind of responsibilities and freedom does he have? Develop entrepreneurship in him? Build emotional involvement? Forget it! How compartmentalized is *your* organization? How much end-to-end responsibility do people in your team have? If the answer is 'not much', what can you do to increase this? Hint: try creating missions that people can handle end-to-end.

had to be present at all times. It was up to them to decide who would be present when.

In a traditional beat, the constables are told where they have to be at each hour, and the SI/inspector would arrive there for a check. This was reversed to 'You do your job. As an officer, I have to find you and will come to wherever you are.' The middle-level officers acted as supervisors and were gradually integrated to the initiative.

The constables were also told that the beat was their baby completely and that they were responsible for it in every way. They could take whatever decisions that were required. If they needed an officer to take a decision, it would be an embarrassment. They could do whatever they thought was best. There were also monetary rewards for nabbing criminals, but these were the same as for the rest of the police force.

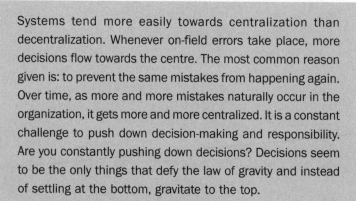

Systems tend more easily towards centralization than decentralization. Whenever on-field errors take place, more decisions flow towards the centre. The most common reason given is: to prevent the same mistakes from happening again. Over time, as more and more mistakes naturally occur in the organization, it gets more and more centralized. It is a constant challenge to push down decision-making and responsibility. Are you constantly pushing down decisions? Decisions seem to be the only things that defy the law of gravity and instead of settling at the bottom, gravitate to the top.

DEALING WITH DILUTION

With the kind of freedom Tripathy gave, how does one ensure that a force used to top-down direction, close supervision and passive-aggressive response patterns doesn't misuse it? There are two kinds of misuse possible: one through shirking, and the other through corruption—cosying up to antisocial elements and taking protection money, the way perhaps some SHOs had done earlier.

Shirking was negated by the tangible and intangible structures and rewards of the beat system. First, there were regular interactions between the SHOs and the beat constables. Twice a day, in the morning and evening, the SI had to meet them to convey information from the SHO and to take back information from the beat to the SHO. Additionally, the inspector or the SHO had to meet them on the beat personally at least once a day. (Each inspector had four to five beats under him.) Further, the assistant commissioner and deputy commissioner had to meet one-third of the approximately twenty-four beats under him once a day—though they usually ended up meeting about 60 per cent of them every day. In addition, night patrols had to cover all sixty beats every night.

Second, each constable on the beat ('beat officer') had a walkie-talkie. And if any distress call was received in their area, they were expected to reach the site before the control room patrol vehicle and police team from the station reached—this soon became a matter of honour.

Third, Tripathy had flashed his mobile number across the city through the local press, TV and radio etc., saying he was available to every citizen for any problem. This ensured that he got constant and quality information from the public. Again, it became a matter of pride for the beat officers to get information before the commissioner got it. Further, complaint boxes were set up in every beat and someone directly from the commissioner's office opened them every day. These mainly contained information about offences, suggestions and information about beat officers.

It was embarrassing for the beat officers if the complaint box contained information they were not aware of.

In addition, Tripathy would meet nearly fifty people a day at his office. They were only too willing to give him feedback on how the beat was working in their areas.

All this ensured that shirking was proactively tackled. However, there were cases where shirking happened, and these beat officers were punished or sent back to station constable status. This was a huge loss of status, and after one or two such examples were made of shirkers, the beat officers did everything possible to retain their superior status.

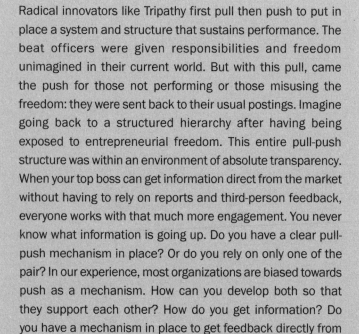

Radical innovators like Tripathy first pull then push to put in place a system and structure that sustains performance. The beat officers were given responsibilities and freedom unimagined in their current world. But with this pull, came the push for those not performing or those misusing the freedom: they were sent back to their usual postings. Imagine going back to a structured hierarchy after having being exposed to entrepreneurial freedom. This entire pull-push structure was within an environment of absolute transparency. When your top boss can get information direct from the market without having to rely on reports and third-person feedback, everyone works with that much more engagement. You never know what information is going up. Do you have a clear pull-push mechanism in place? Or do you rely on only one of the pair? In our experience, most organizations are biased towards push as a mechanism. How can you develop both so that they support each other? How do you get information? Do you have a mechanism in place to get feedback directly from the market?

But perhaps the major factors that contributed to an absence of shirking were intangible. The beat officers commanded tremendous respect and regard in the locality. They were invited for family weddings, asked to inaugurate local events, called to settle disputes, and were generally looked up to. These huge social and community expectations kept them completely engaged and involved.

Tripathy dealt with corruption summarily. Nothing could hinder the implementation of the transformation more than a perception that corruption would be tolerated. When there were complaints about corruption or about officers favouring particular party workers or community members, and CID/special branch verification had shown that the complaints had basis, officers at any level were summarily punished by Tripathy. This included very senior officers. There was absolutely no room for leeway. Corruption meant trouble. Information was so freely available to the commissioner both through direct information and beat feedback that a glaring openness had come into the system, and anything underhand was immediately raised and dealt with. According to Tripathy, he just had to make an example of a couple of people. That was enough to send the message across.

Tripathy also set an example in dealing with the powerful. He dealt summarily with those who broke the law, no matter how powerful they were. And this extended to those who commanded considerable political clout. He once went after a henchman of the ruling political party who was spreading terror in the neighbourhood. This sent the message that nobody was above the law and that the commissioner would take care of those who acted in the interest of the law.

Transformation begins with an enunciation of very clearly defined principles and non-negotiables. There are many dilutors in any transformational mission and corruption is one of the key diluters. Any tolerance of corruption, for instance, would send the wrong signal and the transformation mission would be impacted. Soon, with every instance of winking at corruption, dilution increases and the entire transformation can end up becoming a clone of the original. Radical innovators like Tripathy recognize these dilutors and do whatever necessary to eliminate them. What have been the greatest dilutors in your organization? In the past, what has been tolerated in your organization that has ended up contributing most to dilution? Having identified the dilutors, what are you going to do to eliminate or counter them?

BUILDING INTERNAL MOMENTUM

Initially, the information flow from the beat was directly to Tripathy and he then handed over the information to the inspectors. This was vital to the empowerment of the beat officer and acted as a check on inspectors with a command and control mindset. After the hands-off message had been sent and capability had been built, Tripathy brought in the hierarchy because otherwise this could deteriorate into disciplinary problems. He now asked the beat to inform and report to the inspectors directly. Both knew, however, that information was always reaching the commissioner.

In addition, there were a number of television interviews and newspaper reports about the initiative. In each case, Tripathy allowed the beat officers themselves to talk to the media and share their own stories and examples. It was extremely motivating for the beat officers to see themselves on TV talking about what they had achieved.

Further, Tripathy realized that people from the higher socio-economic categories always spoke only to an inspector when they came into a police station. Constables were never spoken to. Since the beat officer was in charge of the whole locality, he reversed this. Whenever anyone would ask to speak to the inspector about a problem, he was politely redirected to the beat officer. This was reinforced during the weekly Saturday meetings of the beat officers with the community. No inspectors were present. It was just the beat officers and the community. The inspectors were in charge of supervising the functioning of the beat officers under their control, handling investigation enquiries, court work and all other police station duties. The beat was the baby of the beat officers.

There were challenges too. Many cops came to Tripathy and asked him that if streetlights weren't working in their beat, why were they supposed to get them fixed? Wasn't it the job of the municipality? Or why were they supposed to bring plumbers and electricians to people's homes if they had a plumbing or electrical problem? Tripathy had to patiently explain to them that every incident has a crime potential. If streetlights don't work it leads to crime in the dark. If unknown people enter houses in the guise of plumbers or electricians, it can again lead to crime. Over time, as the police began experiencing the love and regard that had built up for them in the community, their mindsets shifted too.

Building External Momentum

Tripathy encouraged the beat to think holistically about the community and not just about policing. He asked that since it was the environment that created criminals, how could it be changed? Soon, it emerged that when the municipal council did not do its civic duties, it affected law and order. Tripathy found that most of the issues that caused anger and alienation were not even related to policing. But when that anger and alienation got expressed through crime and the police used a heavy hand, it caused more anger and alienation in the community—ripe breeding ground for external criminals and terrorists seeking support.

For instance, corruption in getting water supplies, or in the public distribution system, to name a couple of issues, led to considerable anger and alienation. In the case of water supplies by tankers, the problems included tankers not coming on time, small-time rowdies bullying people and making money by 'regulating' the water supply. (Each person was entitled to two buckets but would get only one bucket and be made to pay for it. The remaining water was diverted to hotels and other establishments that paid more for the water.) To deal with this, a beat officer took over responsibility to get the water tanker on time and stood at the distribution point to ensure no payment was asked for and the tanker was emptied and only then sent back.

In the case of the public distribution system, rowdies would bring cars and a number of ration cards and knock off stocks while people stood in queues. This led to resentment against the authorities cooperating with them. Again, a police beat officer stationed himself there and ensured that the PDS stocks didn't get lifted.

Moving Government Departments from Silos and Turfism to Purpose

With this holistic perspective towards community and civic policing, residents began giving the police their applications for water, sewage and telephone connections and these were taken up with the commissioner. This led to a protest by the municipality that the police were overstepping their authority. Tripathy went to the municipal authorities and stated to them bluntly that the residents came to the police because the municipality staff took bribes to do their work. If they did their job fairly and honestly, there would be no need for the police to step in. In one case, he got a crime-prone locality that had no proper road and was involved in brewing illicit country liquor to agree to give up brewing liquor in exchange for a road. But the municipal council did not lay the road. Rather than lose credibility, Tripathy got a local NSS group of volunteers to begin laying the road. They made considerable progress until an embarrassed municipality swung into action and took over. The locality voluntarily stopped brewing illicit liquor.

To drive the holistic community concept further, he took the municipal commissioner and district collector along to visit localities and listen to issues. This helped solve a number of pending civic issues and complaints. Soon, this extended to representatives from other public utilities like telephones and electricity—and eventually to every government department that comes into contact with the public.

Moving Communities from Anonymity and Fragmentation to Familiarity and Cohesion

A regular Sunday meeting is held at every beat attended by the beat officers, the local residents and government departments like the municipality, telephones, electricity, as well as local NGOs. And it's not just about solving government-public issues. It's also important for people to learn how to solve their own conflicts.

As Tripathy says, 'If I can get neighbourhood people to sit together and dialogue for an hour every Sunday, I can surface issues and get them resolved. Even small things like parking a car can cause bad blood.' It's important for neighbourhoods to get together and solve their own problems rather than depend on the police or other enforcers. This meant creating the opportunity for dialogue and building problem-solving skills.

For instance, one neighbourhood complained that school and college girls in their neighbourhood had to go to a bus stop in the next neighbourhood where boys would tease them. The usual response would be to have a plainclothes policeman go there, beat the boys up and put them in jail. But as Tripathy says, that would just spoil the boys' career and you also never know what frame of mind they would come out with and what they would do thereafter. It could actually breed more hatred, more bitterness, and carry the seeds for further violence. Here's an estranged person, easy picking for terrorists or criminals who are always anti-establishment.

So, instead of intervening, the police got members from the other neighbourhood to come for the meeting the next Sunday. When they were informed of the problem, the people of the second neighbourhood said that they would deal with it. They promised that elderly members of the neighbourhood would be personally present when the girls came to the bus stop on their way to and from school and college. No young boy would dare tease a girl in the presence of his parent or an elder. The issue was thus resolved.

The Trichy experiment (as we prefer to call it and not 'community policing' or any other kind of policing) shows that the global paradigm of policing that measures the number of cops per 1000 population as a means of keeping the peace is just an indicative measure. Cops don't have to control the entire population: all they have to do is handle the 3–5 per cent who are criminal. But to do this, they have to *leverage*. And maximum leverage comes when you involve the 95 per cent of the community that is inherently peaceful and law abiding.

The argument for more police is just not good enough if more police means more of the same. In Trichy, 260 cops largely transformed the crime and terror environment. Think about it! Just 260 cops! What Tripathy did was not more policing but shifting mindsets. He shifted mindsets in all the stakeholders: the community, politicians, police, and NGOs. It is this mindset shift that caused the breakthrough.

Orbit shifters don't ask for more resources, manpower or money to make a difference. They take what they have and find a radically different way of using existing resources to make a planet-sized impact. Surat was cleaned up, Trichy was transformed, all without any additional investment of resources.

Tripathy is today an inspector general of police based at Chennai.

And as for Trichy, as he puts it, 'These strategies, introduced during 1999–2001, have produced positive results, both tangible and intangible.' The tangible results show a substantial fall in reporting of crimes against human body, property, etc. The total reporting of crimes of all types have dropped from 11,289, recorded during the year 1999 to 8005 during 2000, which further dropped to 7750 during the subsequent year. Even after seven years, in spite of growth in population, the total number of reported crimes are much below the 1999 mark. Though there was a remarkable fall in reporting of crimes, the city recorded a four-fold increase in registration of cases under 'crime against women', from 40 cases reported during the year 1999 to 160 cases in 2001, possibly due to the increased awareness through the women helpline introduced during August 2000 to enable and empower women victims to come forward and seek justice.

The most satisfying aspect of Tripathy's initiative has been the absence of communal disturbance and an improvement in police performance in terms of increase in the percentage of crime detection and recovery of stolen properties. Police performance in crime detection registered a steady increase from 78 per cent prior to 1999 to 86 per cent in 2000, reaching a peak of 95 per cent in the year 2004. Similarly, the recovery of stolen properties rose from 41 per cent prior in 1999 to 74 per cent in 2000 and reached 90 per cent in the year 2005. In 2007, there was 90 per cent detection of crimes and 87 per cent in recovery of stolen properties. Clearly, Trichy is a very safe place to be in today.

The Trichy experiment has been scaled up in Trichy, Coimbatore and to an extent in Chennai. Ironically, none of the cities most affected by terror—Mumbai, Ahmedabad, Bangalore, or Delhi—have taken it up. Mumbai does have mohalla communities in an attempt to prevent religious riots, but it doesn't have the kind of holistic approach that the Trichy experiment demonstrated. Community policing is seen as just community patrolling. But as the Trichy experiment demonstrates, it is far, far more than that. It is community transformation!

8

CHOLA VEHICLE FINANCE

REMOVING ESCAPE BUTTONS

The most common misconception about innovation is that it's about ideas. Actually, innovation is about aspirations first, people next and finally, about ideas. The most brilliant ideas in the world fail because people haven't bought into them or because the aspirations are tepid.

And when innovation becomes radical in the sense that it takes one to a fundamentally new space, people and aspirations take on an even greater focus. Steve Jobs didn't create the Macintosh with an idea. He created it by inspiring his team to make an 'insanely great' machine. The aspiration was to make something that would redefine the computer age. David Ogilvy didn't create historic ads just by giving ideas. He created them by asking his team to make something immortal.

Closer home, a small unit of a small business within a large company completely redefined itself and set itself on the path of rapid growth and influence when its head, P.N. Vasudevan, understood that in radical innovation, inspiring people and creating aspirations come first and getting ideas comes second.

Chola Vehicle Finance is a division of Cholamandalam Investment and Finance, a company within the billion-dollar Murugappa group of companies that is into a cross-section of industries from finance to fertilizers to steel products. This small division grew at a scorching pace in an industry where most innovations are easily replicated by competitors. From 1998 to 2002, Chola Vehicle Finance grew from an asset base of Rs 140 crore to Rs 800 crore. Today it has an asset base of nearly Rs 4000 crore. And it all started when Vasudevan realized that inspiring people was the key to creating orbit shifts within an organization or industry.

THE BACKGROUND TO INNOVATION

In 1997, Chola Vehicle Finance was a small player in a business where size mattered. Chola was a Rs140-crore company while most of its major competitors in the vehicle finance business both bank-based and non-banking finance company-based had assets of Rs 1000 crore and more. Vasudevan knew that if he had to survive, he had to grow—fast!

But growth wasn't easy. He needed funds for growth and in those days the non-banking finance companies (NBFCs) were under a cloud. A large number had gone under, causing hundreds of thousands of small investors to lose their life savings. And the Reserve Bank of India (RBI), in a bid to regulate, had shut down even more of them. Chola was one of the few that survived the RBI purge. And this was largely because of its risk-averse, cautious approach to finance.

In order to grow, Vasudevan had to go against the very business model that had ensured Chola's survival. He needed to take risks and go after new challenges.

Past success is usually a limiter. In this case, risk aversion had caused the company to survive. People would be congratulating themselves on their risk-averse business model. To now promote risk-taking as a growth paradigm would, in most companies, mean asking for trouble. Pundits tend to immediately arrive with reams of statistics, vital or otherwise, that illustrate how the present business model has served the company well and how a business model similar to the one proposed has ruined other companies.

Purging Legacies through 'Dream Meetings'

Vasudevan did some thinking and realized that rather than opening new branches to achieve growth, he would have to get the existing branches to take on more challenging targets. But doing it the usual way wouldn't work. The usual way, like in any organization, was that he set targets for his branch heads and they argued and battled and sulkingly accepted them when he forced them down. At the end of the year, they always fell short. This had to change. There was no way he could make the growth he wanted through the existing way. They needed to grow at a much faster pace than they were growing now or run the risk of being wiped out by competition. He was sure that only if he could get his team to look at the big picture and excite and energize them, could quantum growth happen.

He began by sharing with each branch the necessity of rapid growth in a dynamic environment in which they were competing with much bigger players. He wrote an exuberant, encouraging letter inviting each branch office to plan its own budgets for the year. This included setting its own sales targets, expenditure budgets, etc., thus giving them complete end-to-end responsibility.

But before putting this into action, he also knew that he had to purge legacies. The team was used to letting others do the thinking for them and take decisions for them. They were used to being supervised. Sudden freedom would be unnerving and could create a drift arising out of a sense of lack of mooring. So Vasudevan began the process of purging legacies through a creativity workshop that helped the team unshackle their minds. After this he invited *each* team to engage with him separately in *dream meetings*. We love that term. It captures perfectly the purpose of a meeting if one has to emerge with anything radical.

In our experience, most target setting is manipulative rather than truly inclusive. The premise that senior management works from is that most people down the line will take the lowest possible target if given a free hand. And therefore there needs to be a show of inclusion and consultation. But all the while there is a target in the top man's mind that he keeps nudging his team towards. He believes that he has been inclusive and has co-evolved the target, but the team feels manipulated. When people say they co-evolve targets along with their team, in many cases they are just being consultative—they ask for opinions and listen to those opinions. But that's not enough. True co-evolution begins when the bosses give up decision-making themselves and allow those down the line to take responsibility for their own work ... end to end!

The purpose of these 'dream meetings' was to break away from the past, to stop looking at what was done the previous year as a reference point for charting the future. The meetings inspired people to explore and explode the market potential and arrive at their aspiration. Vasudevan invited them to set their own quantum growth goals, irrespective of what others in the organization were doing. This process unleashed amazing ambitions and energy among his people. Most branches came through with quantum goals, with 200–300 per cent growth aspirations, and more importantly, the people at the branch level were charged and excited.

The impact of these meetings amazed Vasudevan. Each branch now wanted to go out and capture the market. They had suddenly become masters of their domain, deciding for themselves what their limits were. Vasudevan had managed to unleash the passion that was there in his people.

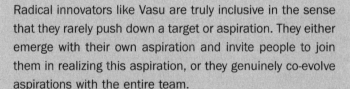

Radical innovators like Vasu are truly inclusive in the sense that they rarely push down a target or aspiration. They either emerge with their own aspiration and invite people to join them in realizing this aspiration, or they genuinely co-evolve aspirations with the entire team.

How do *you* do it? Do you have aspirations or targets? Do you invite people aboard, do you co-evolve aspirations and dream together with your team, or do you nudge people towards your targets? Are you going to do anything differently? When will you begin? The payoffs are huge! How do you get people to dream? What in your leadership style interferes with your people dreaming?

HANDLING DILUTION THE INNOVATIVE WAY

But Vasudevan knew that this wouldn't last. When the rubber hit the road in terms of day-to-day pressures, problems and

> We tend to think of 'motivating' people or 'charging' them or 'empowering' them. And we expend huge energies in trying to do this. It's not about 'motivating' from the outside. It's about triggering the latent passion that is already there within people.

deliverables, the aspiration would get diluted. People would begin to compromise and settle for lower standards. The 200 per cent would become 175 per cent and then 150 … and so on. The immediate would push out the aspiration. And if Vasudevan then began following up and pushing them and reminding them, they would feel discouraged. He knew that he had to do something that would make the effort largely self-sustaining.

Vasudevan now did something radical. He called a press meet and made a public commitment of Chola's new growth targets for the coming fiscal. Now he and his team had to perform or run the risk of losing credibility. There was no going back on the targets without severe embarrassment. Vasudevan had proactively removed all future escape buttons, which would have allowed the 'mission' to slip back in moments of weakness.

He also went to each location and called local press meets, announcing that branch's aspiration. It became very difficult for that branch to slip back now. Their families, friends, and more importantly, their competitors knew their aspiration. They certainly couldn't lose face now.

The impact that these dream meetings and the subsequent press meets had on the employees of Chola was there for all to see. The dream targets were very visibly displayed in every branch in places where they could be seen by customers, dealers, etc. Employees wore badges that had their targets mentioned on them. They were convinced that they could achieve the targets; they lived and breathed the figures. It became a mission in the real sense of the term.

The result was that twelve out of twenty Chola braches achieved their targets. In a market where firms were either stagnating or declining, Chola registered a decent 21 per cent growth rate in the first year, followed by dream growth rates of 60, 85 and 80 per cent. In real terms, it grew from a turnover of Rs 140 crores in 1997–98 to Rs 170 crores in 1998–99, to Rs 270 crores (1999–2000) to Rs 500 crores (2000–01) to Rs 900 crores by 2001–02!

Organizational graveyards are littered with good intentions that have failed through poor execution. And the heart of execution is really about preventing dilution of the strategy or intention. Private internal commitments that we make to the boss or to a customer often get diluted. A public commitment is far more difficult to dilute because one's credibility is on the line.

How many of your private commitments have been diluted? How many times have you settled for 'just enough' when you had originally reached for the moon? If you had removed escape buttons in some way would the quality of your initiatives have been different? What can you do to remove escape buttons in your current project/task?

In organizations there is often a lag of a few years between stimulus and impact. And unfortunately, many organizations are so short-term and immediate gratification based that they pull the plug early when they don't see the stimulus generating results immediately. Fortunately, Vasudevan continued with his initiatives year on year and his growth left the industry growth rate of 15–20 per cent during this period far behind.

CHANGING EXISTING STRUCTURES

But it's not enough just to have dream meetings of course. Once the dream meetings had generated escape velocity within the team and the escape buttons were removed through public commitments, Vasudevan and his team had to change the structures within the organization that maintained the existing state. You can't expect different results without changing the structures that maintain the existing state, because these structures contribute to gravity.

> Structures maintain stability. But they also dictate the direction that you take. Changing these structures involves, in many cases, making paradigm shifts in how the industry operates and paradigm shifts in how the organization operates.

Many internal structures that Vasudevan changed also ended up changing external structures, leading to paradigm shifts. For example, initially the decision on the interest rate at which loans could be disbursed was centrally driven and controlled. After January 2000, this decision shifted to the branches. This shift happened after January 2000 when Vasu asked the branches how they proposed to achieve their dream targets. The branches came up with the idea that they should have autonomy on fixing the rate of interest on individual transactions as long as an overall rate of interest, say 15 per cent, was maintained.

At first, Vasudevan was hesitant about the idea. His concern was that at the beginning of the month, the branches would disburse loans at low rates of interest and at the end of the month they would be unable to meet the target rate of interest. But then he did see the merit of the idea. He also felt that if he did not agree to this, the entire dream target exercise would look like a farce, and could lead to cynicism. As he says, 'There is no point if only the thinking is different; the action has to be different too.' Initially, Vasudevan spent sleepless nights and went through a lot of tension and stress, as his credibility was on the line. But he took the risk and gradually, over the next three years, not surprisingly, the branches settled down very well to this new way. In fact, most branches came up with their own innovative ways of tracking the interest rates.

In our experience, most attempts at radical change fail because leaders aren't willing to give up the structures—the practices that maintain control. It's a frightening thought to let go of control and to trust that those down the line will be as dedicated to the mission as you are. As Peter Drucker says, 'Ninety per cent of what we call "management" consists of making it difficult for people to get things done.' Where are you saying 'no' to your people? Where are you making it difficult for them to get things done? In many cases, the biggest dilution point is the six inches between the leader's ears.

When he decentralized disbursements, Vasudevan also created a paradigm shift in the industry. The earlier industry practice was to have a standardized rate of interest. When he shifted to the weighted average interest rate, Vasu created an industry first. The next logical step was to disburse interest based on customer profiles. The industry practice was to fix standard rates of interest for each class of vehicle finance irrespective of the profile of the customer.

Chola changed this by basing the rate of interest on the risk profile of the borrower. For example, a provision store owner has a higher risk profile than a salaried executive, who denotes a higher risk than a practising doctor. The interest rate charged from each of these three was linked to their risk profiles.

An internal paradigm at Chola was to finance only cars and commercial vehicles. This shifted to financing anything that moves! As a result of this, two new important segments were added to Chola's product portfolio: tractors and two wheelers. In fact, Chola is the first private sector player to enter the tractor finance business.

Additionally, Chola began creating a superior brand image for itself over the rest of the NBFCs. One way it did this was through the quality of its franchisees. Instead of continuing with the traditional model, where a small-time direct sales agent (DSA) becomes a franchisee, Chola began choosing businessmen who had multi-brand two-wheeler showrooms as franchisees, because:

1. These dealerships were usually in prominent locations within cities. Therefore, most people knew where the franchisee was located;

2. The dealerships themselves constituted a captive consumer base for Chola;

3. Since they were full-blown businessmen, their outlook was completely different from those of the traditional DSAs. As a result, they were more receptive to new business ideas.

In order to raise the stakes for becoming a Chola franchisee (and therefore making it a matter of prestige for him), Chola began insisting that the franchisee pay it a deposit of Rs 5 lakh. This was the first time in the industry that people had to pay an NBFC to become its franchisee! Against this deposit, Chola invested Rs 10 lakh of its own and built the infrastructure within the franchisee's premises. As a result, it became a serious business proposition for both parties.

Customer insight was another area that Chola began focusing on when they realized that they had no experience in dealing with two-wheeler and tractor customers. Top executives from Chola took off one week as a holiday and met with customers. The objective was to go to their shops, farms, houses and understand their needs better. For example, the norms used by Chola for providing tractor finance were based on the norms followed by public sector banks. While public sector banks provided loans if the farmer had a minimum of eight acres of land, Chola stipulated a minimum acreage of five per loan. The fact, however, was that Chola had no real basis for determining whether this was the right way of deciding the norm. This was just one example of the kind of issues they resolved by virtue of their customer insight visits.

THE IMPACT

Giving power to the branches ensured that people down the line took on major responsibilities and freed Vasudevan from micro-management of his team. This had a direct impact on Chola's bottom line. It also resulted in a significant change in Vasudevan's role within the organization.

Prior to the dream meetings:

1. Vasudevan set the targets for the branches.
2. All decision-making powers were centralized with him.
3. From the 22nd of every month, Vasudevan couldn't travel as he needed to follow up with all branches regarding their achievements vis-à-vis their targets.
4. He spent 70–80 per cent of his time on routine matters.

After the dream meetings:

1. The targets came from the branches—he just aligned with them on the bottom-line results.

2.   All decisions relating to the branches expenditure were delegated.

3.   He did not need to closely monitor branch performance and therefore, that time was now free and spent on visiting branches and looking for new markets.

4.   He spent 50–65 per cent of his time on business development for the future.

The cumulative impact of all these initiatives was that today, Cholamandalam Investments (Cholamandalam DBS) is one of the largest and most respected NBFCs in the industry. The vehicle finance division is the growth driver for Cholamandalam DBS. And within the Murugappa group, it is now a major player.

> When people dream together they transform industries. Do you dream along with your people or do you dream alone and try to pass on your dreams down the line?

So what does the Chola case tell us about how radical innovators transform organizations?

First, as Vasudevan did, they hold 'dream meetings' that enrol and trigger people to take on impossible challenges.

Second, they remove escape buttons. There is no point in taking on impossible challenges if you leave a back door open to retreat. Then the impossible won't happen. Vasu removed escape buttons through public commitments.

Third, they change the structures—both internal and external—that maintain the existing state. Radical innovation can't happen as long as the existing structures are maintained. Vasudevan gave up central control and moved almost all decisions to the branches. And the results have been awesome.

Vasudevan moved to DCB bank as executive vice president and head consumer banking in end 2005. As of January 2008, Vasudevan set up Equitas Microfinance along with M. Anandan,

ex-managing director of Cholamandalam DBS Finance Ltd and
V.P. Nandakumar, chairman, Mannapuram Group of Companies,
Trichur.

Vasudevan is the managing director of Equitas and the
organization already has several firsts to its credit. Equitas is
today the fourth highest capitalized MFI in the country with a
market capitalization crossing Rs 200 crore. It focuses on the
urban poor rather than on the rural poor and is one of the
fastest growing start up MFIs in the world having already acquired
100,000 clients in nine months, and will end up touching
600,000 families in the first year of operation. Its productivity is
more than three times the best in the industry and a study by
Unitus Advisors, a global microfinance accelerator, shows Equitas
having the lowest cost of acquisition per customer in the industry.
It has introduced many innovations in product features and
processes; for instance, its unique collection 'sticker' process is
protected through copyright.

In true quantum innovator fashion, Vasudevan is on his way
to creating another large success and the lead indicators are
very good.

9

TITAN EDGE

BEATING DEFERENCE

Mahatma Gandhi's greatest struggle in South Africa and in India was not about overthrowing the British. It was about 'How do you make an enslaved race think and feel equal to others when all around there is compelling evidence of the enslaving race's "superiority"?' Britain's superiority was manifest in the very fact that 100,000 British in India ruled 350 million Indians, that it had superior technology, superior guns, machines, products, that it ruled India with its laws, institutions, policies, governance and taxes designed to preserve inequality. In the face of all this, how do you get an enslaved nation to feel equal?

Gandhi's biggest concern was not expelling the British. That could be done. But if it was done without an enslaved people first feeling and seeing themselves as equal to any ruler, one set of rulers would only be replaced by another, and inequality with its inherent exploitation and arrogance would continue. The challenge for him was to get the people of India to move from a state of deference to positive irreverence.

In a sense, Gandhi's challenge is as relevant today. One of the key mindsets that prevent breakthrough product innovation in India is the mindset of deference to the developed world.

THE ORBIT-SHIFTING CHALLENGE

That is the mindset that Titan Watch Industries' then managing director, Xerxes Desai faced, when in 1994, he set his team an orbit-shifting challenge: 'Create the slimmest water-resistant watch in the world!' This meant that the watch would need to be a maximum of 3.5 mm thick—as thick as the edge of a floppy disk—and water-resistant to boot. When they went to the masters of watch making, the Swiss, to look for help and insights, the Swiss said it was impossible. It couldn't be done. A watch could either be ultra-slim or water-resistant. It couldn't be both.

The Titan team, however, took on the challenge and said that if the Swiss couldn't do it, *they* would, and they did. It took them four years, but they did the impossible and they did it through radical feats of engineering that challenged almost every parameter of watch making.

The slimmest water-resistant watch in the world was conceptualized, designed, developed and manufactured not in Switzerland or Japan but right here in India by a company just a little over a decade old then. The 'Edge', as it was called, was production ready by 1998 and was finally launched in the market in 2000. In a very quiet, low-key manner, an Indian company had created an engineering breakthrough and nailed history to its doorstep.

Today, the 'Edge' is a success story for Titan and is sold globally as the world's slimmest water-resistant watch. The single brand contributes to around 6 per cent or Rs 55 crores of Titan Watches' turnover of around Rs 918 crores last year, and to date has sold over 500,000 watches since its launch. But more than the revenue impact, the true impact of the 'Edge' is that it gave

Titan the confidence that it could make truly global innovative products.

TOWARDS A GLOBAL PLAYING FIELD: THE GENESIS

The genesis of the entire story lies way back in 1985 when Titan Watch Industries was set up as a joint venture between the Tata group and the Tamil Nadu Industries Development Corporation. It began with a French collaboration from where they got both the watch movements and the technology to develop them. Commercial production of watches began in March 1987. By 1992, Titan began surpassing the French collaborators and improving on their own creations. Around this time the collaboration wound up and Xerxes Desai then gave the call to design, develop and manufacture a movement from scratch. The larger aspiration was to become a global player. If they had to earn the respect of the best in the world, they had to be technology leaders and not just marketing leaders.

The R&D team anchored by B.G. Dwarakanath created the movement and it was manufactured and put into watches. Then, in 1994, Desai upped the ante. He gave the R&D team the challenge of developing one of the slimmest movements in the world. It fitted in with existing trends towards slim and it was also a tremendous challenge. What would slim mean? Together they set an internal challenge: the movement would be 1.15 mm thin—about as thin as a credit card. This would make it amongst the slimmest in the world if not actually the slimmest. But the challenge would be tremendous. It would actually mean reducing the thickness of the current movement by more than half—from 3.4mm to 1.15mm—an astronomical challenge in any context, but especially in the context of a company that was developing only its second movement in-house.

Desai then upped the ante further. Once the movement was developed, it would have to be put into a case and a watch created out of this. And in India, it would have to be water-resistant. Indians aren't too likely to buy a non-water-resistant watch. That was a further 'impossible' challenge. No ultra-slim watch to date was water-resistant. They were simply not made for the rigours of daily wearing. They were dress watches or concept watches that would go into the watchmaker's in-house or industry museums (literally). But the challenge facing the Titan team was to develop an ultra-slim watch fit for daily rough wear and make it water-resistant.

The Challenges

Developing the 'Edge' wasn't easy since engineering was a huge challenge. But the greater challenges were internal. As B.V. Nagaraj, then head of product engineering, put it, the top challenge was to instil in people the *self-belief* that they could do it. Initially there was lot of scepticism at different levels. The next big challenge was getting enrolment and 'bind' from key people. And the third was the sheer engineering challenge: the design, manufacturing and tooling challenges in both the movement and case. As Nagaraj said, if self-belief and enrolment hadn't happened, the engineering challenge would have been insurmountable.

In something truly radical, the greatest challenge lies always in creating the self-belief in the team. At Titan, the first reaction of many in the organization was, 'If the Swiss can't do it, how can

That is perhaps the biggest illogical conclusion you are going to hear: if somebody else hasn't done it, it always, every time and in every condition means that no one is ever going to do it. And if someone ever does it, it won't be us. It'll be some other team somewhere else.

we?' They concluded that if the Swiss couldn't do it, it couldn't be done.

It was this mindset of deference to the developed world that the key players—Dwarakanath, then chief technology officer, Subramanya Bhatt, then head of movement R&D, Nagaraj and, of course, Desai—had to tackle and it proved to be their greatest challenge when it came to enrolling and energizing the team.

Watches are put together in three main departments: movement manufacture, case manufacture and assembly. Each department had to be enrolled in addition to enrolling members of the R&D team. Enrolled not just to try something out, but to be actual partners in the journey and see it through. For instance, as a team member put it, manufacturing's usual response to anything new is, 'Look boss, you give me the drawing and I'll work as per the drawing. If it works, it works, if not I can't do anything.' But here, once true enrolment and fundamental alignment had happened, the manufacturing team took ownership saying, 'You give it to us and forget about it. We'll look into it and figure out what to do about it and how to make it work.'

> You know true enrolment and alignment have happened when you don't have to follow up with people, and instead leave them alone to do the right thing. Take a look at your colleagues and subordinates right now. If you need to constantly follow up and supervise them, it may mean that fundamental enrolment and alignment have not happened.

THE MOVEMENT CHALLENGE

A team got kicked off within the movement R&D, headed by Subramanya Bhatt and reporting to B.G. Dwarakanath. At that point in time they had absolutely no idea about the kind of benchmarks available in the world. It was more a close-knit group trying to crack the thickness challenge and it had to be done from scratch. From nowhere could they have reengineered the movement.

The challenges were astronomical. To bring down the movement from 3.4 mm to 1.15 mm needed a paradigm shift that threw up a host of technological challenges beginning from design to manufacturing, assembly and testing. For instance, they had to radically miniaturize the size of all components to pack them into the available space of the movement mechanism, specifically the battery and the step motor. Now with the battery, the obvious dilemma was that decreasing the size of the battery would decrease the power backup considerably. It's an either/or challenge. You can either get a battery that's slim or one with a long battery life. You can't get both. But innovation, as we know, is about the 'and'.

All the usual battery suppliers said, 'Impossible! It can't be done.' Through intense secondary research, the team located the only battery supplier in the world (based in the USA) who managed to successfully develop a battery that was only 1.05mm thick and had power backup for a comparatively longer period of time.

But that still wasn't enough. For the watch to be water-resistant over a number of years, it meant that the back cover needed to be removed as infrequently as possible. This obviously meant that the battery would need to be replaced as infrequently as possible and this would only be possible if the battery life was much longer.

If the battery life couldn't be extended dramatically, could the team somehow find a way of reducing power consumption by half? Since the step motor was the heart of the watch and also its biggest power consumer, they would have to find a way to crash the power consumption of the step motor. The step motor is in any case one of the most complicated parts of the movement. Added to this was the challenge of finding a way to reduce power consumption by half!

A silicon chip was developed to extend the battery life and in parallel the step motor was worked on to reduce power consumption. The net effect was that the battery life *doubled*!

A strategic decision was taken by the R&D team to co-design, develop and then outsource manufacturing of the step motor components to Switzerland. All jigs and tools required to assemble the ultra-slim components of the step motor were created in-house.

Think of the attitude of the team. Every block was a challenge to be overcome. As a team member said, every time they went to Desai with an 'insurmountable' challenge, he agreed that it was indeed a challenge. And then asked them, 'What are you going to do about it?' And each time they found options or created them.

The movement was nearing completion. In the journey from conceptualization to development, there were numerous innovations being made in terms of tooling, equipment and production facilities to create one of the slimmest movements in the world. No standards really existed. And if they did, no competing watch company would part with them. Everything had to be developed in-house to micro-micro tolerances. Finally, however, the movement of 1.15mm was ready for use. It would need a case around it and the case would need to be waterproof.

THE CASE CHALLENGE

Once the movement was done, Desai brought in B.V. Nagaraj, head of product engineering, to tackle the casing challenge.

With the working prototypes of the 1.15mm movement,

Nagaraj and Dwarakanath decided to go to Switzerland for the famous Watch Fair in Basel, to meet the Swiss and get them to manufacture a waterproof case for the movement. Like everyone in the watch industry, the Titan team also believed then that the Swiss were the ultimate. As Nagaraj says, 'In the watch industry everything is with reference to the Swiss in terms of style, quality, finish and reliability. If somebody says you are equivalent to the Swiss, it's like the ultimate compliment.'

Given the almost mythical reputation of the Swiss as far as watches were concerned, Dwarakanath and Nagaraj were quite certain that the Swiss would be able to create a waterproof case for their ultra-slim movement. But they were in for a shock. As Nagaraj continues, 'When we spoke to a number of Swiss manufacturers, the first thing they looked at was the movement. They asked us, "Have *you* made it?" They were quite surprised that we had. Then when we spoke about our need for a water-resistant case at 3.5mm overall thickness, a couple of them said we were crazy. A lot of the manufacturers took the prototype back to their factory, came back and said they couldn't do it. We met senior people including VPs, and while they were quite surprised that a company in India could even think of doing this, what was more interesting is that they came back expressing regret that it couldn't be done because it would mean breakthroughs in many components.' The Swiss could manufacture the movement at a stretch, but they couldn't manufacture a waterproof case around it.

The challenges were that the casing had to serve three simultaneous functions: First, it would have to be slim enough to form a maximum thickness of 3.5mm. Second, it would have to be made water-resistant. Third, it would have to be aesthetically good-looking in design parameters as well. Breakthroughs would be required in each of the three main components of a watch case: the top glass, the back cover and the crown (the winding/ adjustment key on the side of a watch).

Take the glass for instance. The thickness is usually 1-1.2mm. For a watch to be 3.5mm thick overall, the glass would have to be 0.3 mm, about the thickness of three sheets of paper. And it would have to withstand the pressures of daily living. It would have to be sturdy enough to handle fairly hard knocks and bumps and be water-resistant as well. At 0.3 mm it meant a 75 per cent reduction in thickness while providing the same strengths and properties as a standard watch glass.

Nagaraj and Dwarakanath came back, had a meeting with Desai and told him the Swiss couldn't do it. Desai asked them his by now famous question: 'What are you going to do? How will you overcome this problem?' They told him, 'Let's build it in-house. If the Swiss can't do it, we will.' Desai replied, 'Let's do it!'

Even though Desai was confident the team could do it, the rest of the organization wasn't. It took time and some visible results before the rest of the organization moved from uncertainty to resolution. But move they did. And ironically, 'If the Swiss can't do it, we will' became the rallying cry. The fact that the Swiss couldn't do it moved from de-energizing the team to energizing it and making it only more resolved to do it right here in India.

> The biggest energy sapper can become the biggest energy booster. They are both often inextricably linked. If you're wondering what your challenge or cause should be, look at your biggest de-energizer. Turn it around, and make it your biggest energizer.

The first challenge that Nagaraj faced was in inspiring his design team. As he says, 'The total design of the watch had to go though a shift. And case design had to go through a complete paradigm shift. We had to break a lot of beliefs around possibility by continuously reminding people that no reference points existed. They would have to create their own reference points.'

They managed to design a case that also had to look aesthetically pleasing all the while, keeping in mind tolerances often as fine as the thickness of a single hair.

The next stage was manufacturing. The chief manufacturing officer, Hari Rao, was very passionate about Indian manufacturing skills. And, as Nagaraj says, he was also very nationalistic in the sense that he wanted India to be at the top in everything. When Nagaraj told him that the Swiss had said it was not possible, Hari Rao said, 'Let's do it and let's take it as a challenge.'

It's a pleasure having people like Hari Rao around. There are often three kinds of people you encounter in organizations: Lead radicals like Hari Rao who instantly take up anything new and challenging; proof seekers who wait and watch, seeking evidence of success before coming on board; and nay-sayers who don't come on board until it's clear that the ship is going full-steam ahead with the new.

But getting Hari Rao on board was just the first step. The bigger challenges were getting the general managers (GMs) of case manufacturing and assembly on board. Rafique Ahmed, the GM of the case manufacturing group, was a very hard-headed, practical kind of person, more inclined to getting the maximum productivity out of the existing rather than trying out something new. Enrolling him wasn't going to be easy. As Nagaraj says, he wasn't the kind to be swayed by new ideas. Hari Rao and Nagaraj spoke to this gentleman about doing something that the Swiss had said was impossible. That struck a chord. Rafique was dead against outsourcing production from a mindset of deference:

outsourcing because people believed we lacked the capability to produce something in-house. He passionately believed that anything could be done in-house. However, in this case, he didn't believe that it would be possible to even make a prototype because the glass was a huge challenge. No glass existed at 0.3mm that could withstand the rigours of everyday wearing. The biggest challenge according to him was the glass. If the design team could crack the glass challenge, he would develop the case for it.

The priority for Nagaraj was now to find a way of 'cracking' the glass challenge. The solution to this problem was found with sapphire glass. Though much more expensive, it was far sturdier and more reliable than glass, and could be made much thinner and still would not break. After a detailed search, they located a niche sapphire glass-making company in Switzerland named Steatlar, which was able to come up with a thin sapphire glass cover for the watch. With the use of this sapphire glass, the first task of finding a very thin glass top was solved. On seeing this challenge cracked, Rafique Ahmed was immediately enrolled.

PROTOTYPE CHALLENGES

Now the prototype challenges began. The biggest challenge they faced was that the metal was so thin on all sides. Fixing the glass so as to ensure it was waterproof was a challenge because in order to maintain the aesthetics of the watch, the thickness of the case between the glass and the edge of the watch had to be in proportion to the thickness of the entire watch. And this meant a thickness of only a few millimetres. Drilling a hole in the case for the crown was another challenge as the metal below the hole was only 0.1mm thick and it kept splitting. Finally, the team figured out a way of doing both. They couldn't reengineer anything because there were no reference points at all. Everything needed to be innovated: new tools for cases, new jigs, everything had to be developed from scratch to deal with the challenges as they arose.

Even the strap was a challenge. The strap was again a paradigm shift. It had to become thin enough to match the edge. The strap supplier had never created a thin strap like that, but today he thanks Titan as he is now able to sell his ultra-thin straps abroad at a premium.

In a true breakthrough product, your partners too get challenged to find new answers and this becomes a competitive advantage for them. When you shift an industry's model and assumptions successfully, by default your partners do so too. The key is to inspire and enrol the partner.

There were several such challenges to be overcome. And one by one they were. Finally, the case was ready and the watch was given for assembly. Assembly again was a major challenge. The clearances came down dramatically between the hands, glass, everything. The team usually worked with 150 microns as clearance. But in this case they had to work with 100 microns—about the thickness of human hair. The challenges multiplied by a factor of ten as very fine clearance between the hands caused them to clash with each other. This needed to be tackled too.

Finally, the watch began to come together. It certainly wasn't easy. As a team member put it, those were extremely frustrating times. 'We used to have big fights and arguments when people would come up and say, "I want to increase the clearance by 50 microns or so." Assembly used to say: I cannot assemble; manufacturing used to say: I cannot manufacture. Each time somebody or the other would say they were not able to work with these tolerances and ask us to increase the tolerances. We had to go and convince people, constantly reminding them that this is the Edge watch, it's not like any other watch. Tell us if you

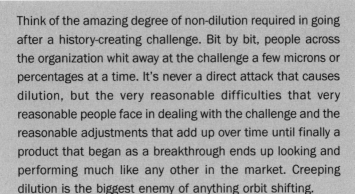

Think of the amazing degree of non-dilution required in going after a history-creating challenge. Bit by bit, people across the organization whit away at the challenge a few microns or percentages at a time. It's never a direct attack that causes dilution, but the very reasonable difficulties that very reasonable people face in dealing with the challenge and the reasonable adjustments that add up over time until finally a product that began as a breakthrough ends up looking and performing much like any other in the market. Creeping dilution is the biggest enemy of anything orbit shifting.

have a problem, we'll help you design jigs and fixtures to solve it. We had to keep reminding the teams that the beauty of the movement would be lost if you couldn't manufacture or assemble it. Imagine if each one of you starts putting your own tolerances, what will happen.'

But then finally, all hard times come to an end and the watch was ready. The Titan team manufactured about fifteen to twenty 'Edge' watches in thirteen different shape variations to be sent to Switzerland for testing.

TESTING

The prototypes were sent for testing to Chronofiable SA, Switzerland, a world-renowned independent Horological Testing Agency. There, the watches were subjected to a series of stringent tests like the high temperature test, low temperature test, Temperature shock, exposure to Vibrations of 50 hertz to 150 hertz, shock tests, bump tests and drop tests etc, all spread over a period of eight weeks. After these tests, the Titan Edge was certified as not just reliable, but also water-resistant up to thirty metres.

They were also tested at Titan internally, and what's interesting is the way Dwarakanath tested it. He says, 'Sure the agencies test thoroughly. But somehow they can never replicate actual life conditions.' So he has what he calls the wall test, the floor test, the pool test and the Bangalore-Hosur road test. What this gentleman does is throw the Edge against a wall, and on the floor at different angles to check if it stays safe. He chucks it into a swimming pool and it's expected to work. Finally he ties it to the shock absorbers of his car and makes several trips on the terrible roads between Bangalore and Hosur, covering 200 km in all. The 'Edge' passed these tests too.

The team had done the impossible. They had nailed history to their doorstep and created the world's slimmest water-resistant watch. And it all started with Xerxes Desai's orbit-shifting challenge to create the slimmest water-resistant watch in the world. A team that believed it didn't have the competency suddenly discovered talents they had no idea they had.

SECTION IV

COMBATING DILUTION

Entropy, the gradual wearing out and breaking down of everything, is one of the strongest laws of the world we live in. According to the second law of thermodynamics, energy or heat naturally flows from an object of higher concentration to one of lower concentration; matter, too, deteriorates from a state of higher organization to that of lower organization. In other words, entropy or dilution is the natural order of things. An innovation mission is often faced with resistance and the drive to go back to the status quo. It takes constant vigilance to make sure that entropy or dilution doesn't creep in.

And dilution can creep in at every pivot, several times a day. Faced with resistance, there may be the pressure to reduce the out-of-the-box to a within-the-box challenge. Look at Shantha Biotech. It constantly battled dilution and produced a vaccine at Rs 30–40 per dose against all odds. But when they wanted to market the vaccine, they found that the existing structures of trade wouldn't allow them to. After commissions to the super stockist, stockist, retailer, doctor and to the marketing organization, the cost of the vaccine would be Rs 500 a dose. This was a key dilution point. Rather than accept this, Shantha and Varaprasad found an alternate delivery channel. They roped in doctors to create vaccination camps where the vaccines were sold at Rs 50 a dose.

Jaideep Bajaj, a sales manager with Johnson and Johnson at Delhi, saw an ad from Maruti some years back, calling for help and tenders in creating first-aid kits to go with each new car. He met the Maruti officials and together they evolved what the kit should contain. He went back to his boss to tell him that they could supply to Maruti. His boss said, 'Nothing doing. We're in the pharma business, not in the car business.' And what's more, Maruti wanted a certain product that they didn't have, so nothing doing. Most of us would have given up here. But Jaideep went back to Maruti and again co-evolved a kit that Johnson and Johnson could supply end to end. He went back to his boss who again said, nothing doing. The bandage roll size that Maruti wanted was too small and Johnson and Johnson didn't have that Stock Keeping Unit (SKU). Jaideep didn't quit. This time he went to J&J's largest distributor in Delhi and proposed to him that he set up a facility to make a new SKU against a guaranteed order. The distributor agreed. The first-aid kit was sold through the distributor. Jaideep's annual sales were Rs 6 crores per annum. With this single deal and contract for four years, they went up to Rs 10 crores per annum. Talk about pay-offs!

What operating principles do people who combat dilution follow? Perhaps the key operating principle is one of 'no compromise on the aspiration'. Priya at Erehwon refuses to accept that something can't be done. Her constant refrain is to constantly ask: 'What's in my control that I can do?' And she does it. Rajiv Narang's key operating principle when faced with dilution is: 'It has to be done. The only question is how to do it.'

There are a number of operating principles that different people work with. For instance, K.N. Das of Tata Refractories has an operating principle of 'one more time'—every time. And it's always just one more time till he gets the breakthrough.

S.R. Rao of Surat has an operating principle of what he calls 'character'. When faced with any difficulty, he asks himself: 'What's the right thing to do? What does it take character to do?' And often he finds 'character' means persisting in the face of almost insurmountable odds.

In the biographies of the three orbit-shifting missions that follow, Shantha Biotech, Su-Kam and the Surat transformation, each orbit shifter overcame immense challenges and gravities that threatened to pull the initiative apart.

10

SHANTHA BIOTECH

UNLEASHING BIOTECHNOLOGY IN INDIA

More breakthroughs come from upset people than from market studies or organizational objectives. Kennedy got angry when the Soviets went to space first, Gandhi got upset when he was thrown out of the train compartment at Maritzburg, J.N. Tata got upset at British discrimination against Indians and man went to the moon, a country was born, and India's steel and hotel eras began.

Varaprasad Reddy is a furious man. And it's good that he's furious. Because his fury created the biotechnology revolution in India.

In 1991, nearly 340,000 people were dying of Hepatitis B in India every year because the cost of the vaccine, at Rs 750 per dose and nearly Rs 2250 for an entire course of three vaccines, was prohibitively expensive for the vast majority of Indians. So while the West was more or less completely inoculated from Hepatitis B, it was rampant in the developing world. Countries like India needed the vaccine far more than the developed world did. And yet the cost of a vaccine that would be used mainly by third world countries was so prohibitive that that they couldn't afford it. This sorry state of affairs continued for a decade or so after the vaccine had been commercially produced. And there was no reason to believe that it wouldn't continue in the same way for another decade or more.

But then one man, a radical innovator, came into the picture with a background not in vaccines but in batteries and electronics—and he crashed the price of a vaccine dose from Rs 750 to Rs 50! A course cost only Rs 150 as against Rs 2250 earlier. Globally, prices crashed and today the vaccine is sold for as little as Rs 15. In India, the number of vaccinations per annum rose from 80,000 in 1991 to more than 100 million in 2008!

Varaprasad, in the process of achieving his dream, humbled a powerful MNC and impacted the global prices of the Hepatitis B vaccine.

OBSESSIONS OF AN ANGRY INNOVATOR

It takes obsession to make the impossible happen. When Varaprasad embarked on his obsession in 1991, India was still the backwaters of the world. Narasimha Rao had just opened the economy and nobody believed that India could do much with its baggage of red tape, poor resources and near bankruptcy. But Varaprasad put together a bunch of passionate, obsessed people who made magic happen and created a high-tech vaccine that pulled India kicking and screaming into the biotechnology age. And it all started with Varaprasad Reddy getting infuriated ...

Varaprasad was already infuriated when he flew to New Jersey in the US to spend some time with his cousins there. He had just been cheated out of his business by a partner and he went to the US for a break and for some peace and quiet. One of his cousins was going to Geneva for an international health conference and Varaprasad tagged along because he 'wanted to see the Alps'.

We don't know if he ever got around to seeing the Alps, but he did see something at the conference that made him furious. He saw Indians being treated very badly by the westerners there. India needed vaccines and couldn't afford them, so they would go to these conferences and ask for free or subsidized vaccines. The western countries would speak of them in a belittling manner: 'Here come the South Asians, begging bowl in hand. How long can the West carry the burden of their teeming millions?' Comments and snide remarks were being made all the time though no one seemed to mind. But Varaprasad was upset. And he decided he wanted to do something to change this.

The rest of the third world was inured to the remarks of the westerners. Nobody seemed to mind. But one man who came in from the outside heard what they had to say and got infuriated. That's one of the characteristics of radical innovators. They take things personally and do something about it. They are not restricted to the status quo of 'we are like this only'. When you hear peeves and complaints against your company, what do you do? Do you shrug them off as something 'they' always say? Or do you get infuriated enough to do something about it?

At Geneva, Varaprasad also heard about Hepatitis B for the first time. He went back to India, found out more about Hepatitis B's impact and decided he was going to produce the vaccine in India. The easiest way to do this was to get a technology transfer. He went back to his cousins in the US who were familiar with US businesses and asked them to point out a company. They told him: 'Go west young man'—to California, to the headquarters of a leading genetic engineering firm.

So Varaprasad went to the Wild West. He didn't meet any Red Indians, but he did meet someone at the firm who told him that the technology he wanted was too advanced for Indians, too expensive for India, and why did he want it anyway? There were so many people in India that a few thousand deaths didn't matter. If Varaprasad was angry earlier, this made him really furious. He got up fuming and told the man that he'd develop the vaccine indigenously within two years and show him just what could be done in India by Indians.

Varaprasad went back to NJ and asked his cousins and friends to organize a meeting of as many Indians in biotechnology in the US as they could get together. They did that. At the meeting of about thirty to thirty-five people, Varaprasad narrated the story of what had affected him and made an impassioned plea saying that he wanted to do something monumental. He said he had a dream. He wanted to eliminate Hepatitis B from India.

While his audience was moved by his passion, they smiled when he said that he wanted to make a high-tech r-DNA or recombinant DNA vaccine in India.

Those humouring, indulgent smiles had Varaprasad hopping mad. He told them, 'What kind of Indians are you? You have been educated by India, even now you look to India for your cultural and spiritual needs. What are you giving back to your country? Is your involvement to the country

In our experience one of the key hallmarks of a radical innovator is that he manages to get people on board by appealing to their emotions and aspirations. He goes beyond the logical and reaches parts that no rational appeal can. Like Varaprasad did, or Steve Jobs did in another context, when he famously asked John Sculley, 'Do you want to sell sugared water for the rest of your life or do you want to change the world?'

that's given you so much limited to asking for pickles and gongura chutney from home?' This made the audience sit up. And this started the process of India entering the biotechnology age.

The scientists were so moved by Varaprasad's passion and dream of eliminating Hepatitis B from India that they promised to find people in the US who could train a team if Varaprasad managed to put one together in India. Varaprasad also managed to get them to put up Rs 120 lakhs for the cause. Varaprasad now had some money and a promise of help if he could put together a team in India.

Varaprasad believed so passionately and deeply in his cause that he was able to inspire others to believe in it with him. On the other hand, most others we meet did believe passionately about something once. But over time they allowed that passion to dry out and have now become just another brick in the wall. What's your dream? What's your passion? Is it still there? What are you doing about it?

ENROLLING FOR THE DREAM IN INDIA

Varaprasad came back to Hyderabad with some money and a dream. Now the challenge was to find people in India who could make it happen. But how would he put together a team of people to do something that had never been done before? How could he get them to buy into his dream? Did the skilled manpower even exist? His background was in electronics engineering. He had no clue about biotechnology. But that didn't stop him.

He began looking around for people and institutions for help and guidance and went to Osmania University in Hyderabad.

Dr Malla Reddy, the vice chancellor of Osmania, was impressed by Varaprasad's cause, his energy and passion. He agreed to allow Varaprasad to conduct research in the university's microbiology department. Varaprasad would spend Rs 5 lakhs to upgrade the lab for his work. In return, he would get full use of the lab. What would have cost Varaprasad Rs 20,000 a month was settled for a one-time payment of Rs 5 lakhs.

At Osmania, he was introduced to Dr Gita Sharma who was a reader in the microbiology department. She had earlier worked with world-class scientists at the University of Rochester, New York, doing research on interferons—proteins in the body that assist the immune system by inhibiting the reproduction of viral cells. She told Varaprasad that r-DNA was a good area to get into and he asked her to identify a project for this. She suggested interferon, as that was her specialty. Varaprasad said he would support her in her interest and then suggested Hepatitis B. Dr Gita joined up and agreed to direct the lab work. They would work on both interferon and Hepatitis B.

Dr Gita became one of his first and perhaps most committed crusaders. She came in because Varaprasad showed her how together they could make both their dreams come true.

By giving Dr Gita the freedom to pursue her own dream, Varaprasad got her help to pursue his dream. Varaprasad created a very symbiotic relationship. Radical innovators create symbiotic relationships that bring in supporters. They enrol people by finding ways in which the other person's dreams can meld with their own. People will go with you to the ends of the earth if you can show them how the journey will help them to achieve their dreams.

Dr Gita began recruiting scientists and bio-technicians for the lab. She began putting together a list of items required, and machines started arriving. But the team still needed help and guidance. Towards the end of 1992, Varaprasad's cousins put him in touch with Dr Guntaka Rami Reddy, a brilliant microbiologist working at Columbia University. Varaprasad phoned him and he agreed to help out the team in India. He got so involved that his wife began complaining to Varaprasad about the phone bills to India.

Varaprasad kept finding supporter after supporter—people awed by his dedication and by the boldness of his vision. Shantha Biotechnics got off the ground in the year 1993. It is named after Varaprasad's mother Shantha who had always advised him to go into businesses that have a social impact.

In early 1993, Varaprasad met Dr Guntaka in person to discuss the venture in detail and Dr Guntaka was even more inspired to help out. Imagine this: a person with no background in biotechnology inspiring a widely respected scientist in the field who had worked on a Noble laureate's team. Dr Guntaka offered his lab in Columbia.

In August 1993, Dr Gita left for Dr Guntaka's lab on leave from Osmania. She began work on isolating the surface antigen (the gene that creates the shell that covers the Hepatitis B virus). She had never done something like this. But Varaprasad had faith in her.

All vaccines comprise this surface antigen that provokes a response from the body's immune system to destroy the virus. The challenge was to separate the surface antigen and implant it into another organism that produces the surface antigen but not the virus itself. This enables the antibodies to be produced in enough quantities to destroy the Hepatitis B virus if it enters the body at a later date. The recombinant technology that basically combines the DNA of two organisms—a host and a bacteria so that the bacteria gets an additional DNA trait that allows the human body to develop immunity to it—was comparatively recent and quite challenging. While the steps in the production were known in principle, the actual manufacturing process was a secret.

It took four months. The antigen was isolated and Dr Gita returned to India in December 1993.

Combating Dilution

For Varaprasad, the research was taking its toll. Two years had passed, money was running out. His father sold his lands and that too wasn't enough. Varaprasad went from pillar to post. No Indian bank had heard of biotechnology back then. The chairman of a nationalized bank told him to 'get out and stop wasting my time'. Venture capitalists demanded huge chunks of equity that would have effectively left Varaprasad as an employee. All doors seemed closed, and the lab required more money for the next stage—for a clean room, high-tech machines, reagents etc.

Things were looking really bleak. Varaprasad and his project were in trouble after so much had been done, but then, as so often happens, help came in from an unexpected source. Oman's foreign minister was scouting for investment opportunities. His representative, Mr Khalil, was in India looking for opportunities to invest in Indian entrepreneurs fired with zeal and he heard of Varaprasad's dream. They met in Mumbai. Khalil was extremely impressed by Varaprasad's passion for a social cause.

He was also impressed by the quality of support that Varaprasad had assembled to make his dream happen. The Omani foreign

Radical innovators like Varaprasad knock on so many doors, meet and inspire and battle so many people that they actually begin to create ripples in the fabric of the universe. Momentum begins to build ... and that's when things happen, seemingly by luck or accident.

minister put up Rs 190 lakhs and arranged loans from the Bank of Oman at liberal terms. Varaprasad had gone full steam ahead, money or no. And the money came.

But now on the project side things were limping along. All those Varaprasad had assembled were scientists who had done pure research. Never any development. They had never worked on a product. So while the scientists were enthused about the research, Varaprasad needed a product. Time was running out. He was putting up a new state-of-the-art factory for production. No expertise existed in India for setting up such a factory. Again Varaprasad's inspiring cause, passion and energy paid off. People literally came from across the world to help out, staying at Varaprasad's home. And the factory began coming up. 'I made appeals, wrote letters, was called for lectures, spoke, met people … never gave up.'

By the end of 1994, as the factory was coming up, differences were cropping up between doctors Gita and Guntaka. Dr Gita was against the use of e-coli that Dr Guntaka was recommending, as she believed this would lead to regulatory problems later. But she wasn't able to come up with an alternative. Varaprasad was under pressure to do something. He was torn. On the one hand he was grateful to Dr Gita for being the first scientist to come on board, on the other hand, time and money were running out. Osmania University took the matter out of his hands. There were some administrative problems and they were asked to vacate the lab.

Dr Guntaka put Varaprasad in touch with the Centre for Cellular and Molecular Biology (CCMB) in Hyderabad. CCMB agreed to give its lab to Shantha Biotechnics for twelve months until Shantha's own factory was ready. Dr Gita was in a fix. She could either take a long leave of absence from the university or resign and join Shantha, neither of which was feasible for her. She reluctantly handed over charge to Dr K.S.N. Prasad at CCMB. In October 1995, Shantha moved to its own factory. CCMB seconded Dr Prasad to Shantha for a year as the R&D consultant.

The first batch of r-DNA vaccines was ready in March 1996. Testing was done on animals. Then Phase I trials—the first stage in human testing to test for safety and tolerability of a drug— were done by the Nizam's Institute of Medical Sciences in Hyderabad. Varaprasad was the first volunteer for the test, along with his family and eighteen of the company staff. His team still talks about this a decade later. How he had faith in them and stood first in line for the testing. This is the stuff legends are made of!

In December 1996, Phase II clinical trials to assess how well the drug works were conducted by Nizam's Institute of Medical Sciences in Hyderabad and King Edward Memorial Hospital in Mumbai.

The results were out in April 1997. Shanvac came out with flying colours.

On 18 August 1997, Shanvac, India's first r-DNA vaccine was released into the market by Renuka Choudhary, the then Union health minister. But the battle had only just begun ...

DEALING WITH COMPETITION

If dealing with an insensitive bureaucracy was tough, dealing with a ruthless competitor who saw the market as too small to be shared was even tougher. Sensing the impact the 'Swadeshi' vaccine was going to make, the MNC market leader of the Hepatitis B vaccine in India brought down its price from Rs 750 to Rs 520. But that wasn't all. Rumours began floating around that the Indian vaccine wasn't safe.

Economic forces also worked against Shantha. With its margins, the MNC was able to give higher commissions to the doctors, and to Shantha's dismay they found that a lot of doctors were in cahoots with the MNC and were propagating the MNC vaccine and the alleged non-safety of Shanvac.

Shantha then took up the matter with the Drug Control Authority—after all, their certificate of Shantha's efficacy was being questioned. After a series of comparative tests across six centres between the MNC product and Shanvac-B, the Shantha vaccine produced better results. Results for vaccines are measured under two parameters:

(i)   Antibody titre: this is the percentage of antibodies triggered by the vaccine. The higher the number of antibodies, the more efficient the vaccine.

(ii)   Protection: what per cent of the vaccinated are actually protected—there's always a percentage that doesn't get protected. The attempt is to make this as small as possible.

Both vaccines scored the same in protection, but Shanvac scored higher in antibody titre. After the results were published, around 200 doctors rallied for Shantha and its product. The international and widely respected journal *Vaccine* took up the issue and published the results, silencing the sceptics.

THE MARKETING CHALLENGE: IMPOSSIBLE TO SELL BELOW RS 519 ...

The next big challenge was in marketing. The marketing department of a major Indian pharma company said that since the MNC vaccine was priced at Rs 520, Shanvac should be 'strategically' priced at Rs 519, and it projected sales of Rs 50 lakh, Rs 75 lakh, and Re 1 crore over three years. When Varaprasad asked them why these figures, they said that this was based on their experience of the maximum a new product could sell.

But neither the rates nor volume projections matched Varaprasad's dream. His dream was to make a vaccine affordable to the common man. He wanted to price it at Rs 50 and inoculate at least 10 per cent of children in India right away. He would market it himself.

Shantha began recruiting people for the marketing effort. The only criterion was a sense of pride in selling a Swadeshi product. A doctor offered to train the recruits and the effort started. Because of the publicity Shanvac-B received, people became aware of the dreaded disease, Hepatitis B, but the benefit went to the existing market leader.

So, like everything else, this too ran into rough weather. Sales weren't picking up. Besides collecting huge margins from MNCs, doctors were found to be using Shanvac-B, but collecting MNC vaccine rates from the patients, telling them in the process, that the swadeshi vaccine was no good. Further, while the vaccine was being marketed for Rs 50, it was finally hitting retail shelves at Rs 180 after the commissions of super stockists, stockists, retailers and doctors' commissions from the retailers.

Again Shantha persisted and overcame the problem without diluting the objective. Varaprasad realized that a vaccine didn't really need a prescription and anyone could ask for it. He wondered how they could eliminate the middlemen—in this case the doctors. He went to the Indian Medical Association (IMA) and told them that we have an Indian vaccine at lower cost and it is not being used. They invited him to give a lecture to the association and he got tremendous support there. Together they hit on the idea of direct contact and decided to organize mass-vaccination camps. There were again protests and blocks, this time from the pharma associations and trade unions. But with the help of the IMA, camps were conducted on a never-before scale. In one particular camp, nearly 40,000 people came for vaccination. There were people queuing up for a shot. Once again, Shantha had overcome.

Shantha ended up selling the vaccine at Rs 50 and earned revenues of Rs 8 crores the first six months, Rs 23 crores in the first year, Rs 32 crores in the second and Rs 36 crores in the third year. By the end of March 2009 they hope to cross Rs 210 crores.

The number of immunizations has increased from 80,000 to over 100 million per year. The cost of Shanvac-B is now Rs 15, in keeping with Varaprasad's commitment of reducing costs to the end consumer.

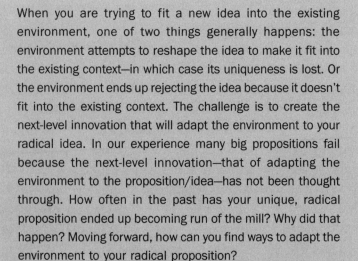

When you are trying to fit a new idea into the existing environment, one of two things generally happens: the environment attempts to reshape the idea to make it fit into the existing context—in which case its uniqueness is lost. Or the environment ends up rejecting the idea because it doesn't fit into the existing context. The challenge is to create the next-level innovation that will adapt the environment to your radical idea. In our experience many big propositions fail because the next-level innovation—that of adapting the environment to the proposition/idea—has not been thought through. How often in the past has your unique, radical proposition ended up becoming run of the mill? Why did that happen? Moving forward, how can you find ways to adapt the environment to your radical proposition?

As Varaprasad says, 'Unlike the Indian pharma majors, I could never think of why it [shaping the environment] could not happen. For me, ignorance turned out to be an advantage.' For India too.

Today Shanvac is a vaccine that is being used by the WHO and is now also selling in the US.

Shanvac is the first WHO pre-qualified Hepatitis B vaccine from India. Only four other vaccines have had this honour so far: one from the US, two from Korea and one from Belgium. At one point, 52 per cent of Unicef vaccines were supplied by Shantha.

By all accounts Varaprasad should be a happy man today. He's come out on top, done the impossible and brought out a high-tech vaccine from India. He has broken mythical 'impossible' barriers and in the process has been the inspiration for a slew of Indian biotech firms who are now doing very well. Vaccine prices in India have dropped from Rs 780 a dose to about Rs 20. Varaprasad should certainly be satisfied. But … 'I haven't yet achieved my goal. Hepatitis B hasn't been totally eliminated from India. Until the task is accomplished, I won't consider myself to be successful.'

In the meantime, the warrior joined the next battle—against another big killer, cancer. The objective: bringing down the cost of Interferon drugs that enable the patient to fight back cancer from Rs 3000 a dose to just Rs 400. The same kinds of battles with the bureaucracy, fixed mindsets and established market leaders ensued until the product, Shanferon, was finally launched. Shanferon is claimed to be the only Interferon Alpha 2b in the world to be cloned and expressed in Pichia pastoris, a eukaryotic new-generation host. In other words, according to the company it is the only yeast-derived vaccine in the world and has fewer and milder side effects than the e-coli derived products.

THE ORGANIZATION

What's Shantha the organization like? What kind of people make up the organization?

Take K.V. Sudhir, senior scientist at Shantha. He was one of the four who initially joined at Osmania University. As a microbiologist and lecturer, he had a slew of jobs to choose from. But he decided to join Shantha because he says, 'I was a rebel. And I didn't want to work in some organization and become a faceless cog. I wanted to make a difference.'

When he started, there was nobody to guide them. Machinery that had come in were so high-tech that the local installers had no idea what to do with them. Sudhir and his colleagues had to read the manuals and then install the machinery themselves. Everything was zero-based.

When Shantha started operations, the first batch of scientists they interviewed and selected didn't join. They either didn't consider Shantha to be up to their expectations, or were not up to the challenge. The four who did come in were attracted by the

Never underestimate the early supporters. They may not be the ones you were originally looking for. They may not be your first or even second choice. But when you are starting off, these early supporters who come on their own are invaluable. An orbit-shifting challenge in its initial stages often needs more passion than skill. Passion overcomes obstacles. The early supporters join because of their passion for your cause. You can't beat passion. They may not necessarily be the 'best', but they create the conditions for the best to join later. If forced to make a choice between skill and passion, choose passion every time. It's the key differentiator.

prospect of working in a new, challenge-based environment, 'doing something that had never been done before in India'.

Sudhir says he gets stifled by routine, which is why he is happy working at Shantha. Varaprasad keeps throwing new challenges at the team that forces them to rethink completely. For example, he told the team that he wanted to produce Interferon and sell it at Rs 150 when the market rate was Rs 2400. This was a challenge that forced the team to rethink everything from scratch, and eliminate all waste–process and raw material. Today Interferon sells at Rs 300 from Shantha.

What motivates Sudhir is the core philosophy of the company: 'Human health care products affordable to the common man.' And the common man in India is different from the common man in the US.

Other factors that motivate him are the fact that at Shantha he works with no interference, and that there's tremendous respect for initiative and innovation—failures are not frowned upon. This actually puts added pressure on individuals. As Sudhir recounts, he had washed a fermenting machine with weak acid to clean it. But then found to his horror that the acid had eaten away at the linings of the machine. Nothing was said to him, and a new machine was ordered. It took four months to come because it was imported. Those were the most painful four months of his life. Work had stopped, but nothing was mentioned to him at all and this really put great pressure on him to ensure that something like this didn't happen again. Since then, he says, he's never operated a machine without first carefully reading the manual.

Mistakes are never frowned upon. Failing to report them however is. People have been dismissed for covering up of mistakes. Cover-ups mean user lives can be lost. That's unacceptable.

S.V. Kotbagi, vice president of operations, says that emotions play a major role in the organization. The organization was born out of emotion when Varaprasad felt insulted at the disparaging remarks he heard. According to him, Transgene, another company, had earlier tried to produce Hepatitis B vaccine in India with the advantage of transfer of technology, but had failed. As he says, 'Transgene had a farsighted approach, but they couldn't do it. Shantha had an emotional approach. Once an emotional goal is in place, everything follows—strategies, people, resources, tools.'

Today, emotions are tapped even in workmen by constantly sharing with them the impact of what they do. They are told, for instance, how a single mistake or carelessness can come back to haunt their own families if a defective product is bought by them.

In addition, to help them see the larger picture, multitasking is done. Every person has to know more than three other tasks. In most cases, they know the end-to-end operations and work in each area. Many companies don't do this for fear that the individual will leave and take his knowledge to competing companies. But at Shantha, the individual's satisfaction is more important. 'If emotional satisfaction is not present,' as Kotbagi says, 'the organization needs to depend on standardizations, methodologies to maintain effectiveness.' Shantha doesn't need to.

> In a fast changing world, your organization will need to continually reinvent itself. Do you have the kind of people who can do that? How many passionate, obsessed people do you have in your organization? If you don't have too many, what are you going to do about it?

Shantha the organization is stuffed with passionate and obsessed people. People who believe they can walk on water. Who can deal with any challenge that emerges or is thrown at them.

Varaprasad, the Battler

For Varaprasad, everything started with the thought that there are things that should be done but are not. And that bugs him. He says that vaccines should save lives, but they don't save as many as they can because pharma companies are focused on profits. As he says, he produced Shanvac at Rs 50 not through a major tech breakthrough but because he refused to charge the 3000 per cent profit that others charged. 'We are in the business of saving lives, not of selling vaccines for profit.'

As a guiding philosophy, Shantha will manufacture everything that fulfils three criteria:

(i)   The product needs to be imported;
(ii)   It improves the quality of life; and
(iii)   The cost of the product is high and prevents the common Indian from benefiting from it.

How has Varaprasad made the impossible happen over and over again? According to him, all he does is to disagree with the belief that something can't be done. He draws inspiration from a line in the Gayatri mantra that says, 'Let the good task begin; everything will be alright.'

As he says, 'People from the biotech industry knew for sure why something couldn't be done. I'm not from the industry therefore I didn't know why it couldn't be done. For me, if other vaccines can be available at Rs 15, why can't a Hepatitis B vaccine be available at Rs 50—three times more? Therefore I just went ahead and did it.'

If there is a key lesson that Varaprasad's story tells us, it's to dream the impossible and go after it. At every stage there are choices—the choice to drop out, the choice to go forward by accepting dilution, or the choice to go forward without dilution. Varaprasad consistently dreams the impossible and chooses to go ahead without dilution. What have your dreams and choices been?

Varaprasad says he found support from people through making appeals, writing letters, giving lectures at any forum he got a chance to speak at. And people rallied around to help him. As he says, 'I can smell out those who have a hunger to do something for the country.'

Internally, he recruits looking first for attitude and hunger for growth. His people have a major say in the running of the company. As he says, he's not a biotechnologist or expert. In Shantha there's no boss, no leader. We're all one, they say. Shantha's team is closely involved with Shantha through stocks, ESOPs and profit sharing. As Varaprasad says, 'We all have social obligations. And we need to fulfil them.'

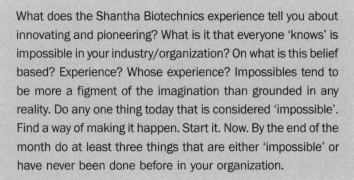

What does the Shantha Biotechnics experience tell you about innovating and pioneering? What is it that everyone 'knows' is impossible in your industry/organization? On what is this belief based? Experience? Whose experience? Impossibles tend to be more a figment of the imagination than grounded in any reality. Do any one thing today that is considered 'impossible'. Find a way of making it happen. Start it. Now. By the end of the month do at least three things that are either 'impossible' or have never been done before in your organization.

Currently, Shantha Biotechnics is one of the most admired companies in the biotechnology space in India and has a host of products in its kitty as well as in its pipeline of forthcoming products. A French company called Merieux Alliance recently picked up a stake in Shantha by buying out the Omani stakeholders' shares, and Shantha is now a part of Merieux Alliance, though it continues to be headed by Varaprasad Reddy.

And it all began with Varaprasad getting upset and refusing to let difficulties or gravity bog him down.

How much gravity have you battled in the past? Have your big ideas become diluted? Which forces of gravity diluted them: individual, organizational, industry, country or cultural? There is no point sitting back and complaining about 'the system'. Gravity exists. It's real. Find ways of battling it. All that stands between you and that historic impact you may want to create is a couple of these five forces. Battle them. Varaprasad battled the two toughest gravities—country and culture. If he can do it, so can you. 'Let the good task begin.'

11

THE SURAT TRANSFORMATION

URBAN RENEWAL

Orbit shifts happen when planets, countries, cities, organizations and individuals change an existing track and move into a completely different orbit. Steve Jobs joined a group of techies designing a 'user-friendly' computer and reframed the challenge from making a 'user-friendly' machine to an 'insanely great' one. And the great Macintosh was born that changed the orbit of the computer age. Closer home, a municipal commissioner in Patna, S.K. Singh, found that existing property tax assessment methods created opportunities for huge harassment. He asked himself, 'How can I make this foolproof and so transparent that it leaves no scope for assessors' "discretion"?' He took a bloated 256-page document that had existed for half

We spend our lives waiting for that big opportunity, that big break. And it's there all the time—waiting for us. All we needed was to take what we have in hand and use it to make a delta change. Look around you. Every sign of progress you see anywhere has happened because some individual didn't see himself as doing 'just a job'. What can you do to make a delta change today?

a century and reduced it to one and a half pages—and implemented it in the face of huge opposition. Today, his transparent model is becoming the standard across the country with the governments of Uttar Pradesh, Madhya Pradesh and Tamil Nadu adopting similar models. In Surat, a bureaucrat took over a plague-ravaged city and shifted its orbit to make it the second cleanest city in the country.

What does it take to shift orbits? In many cases, orbit shifters are ordinary people who make a quantum difference not by switching over to a different job or by asking for a big project, but by doing their present job differently. Take S.R. Rao and Surat. For decades, Surat was one of India's filthiest cities. S.R. Rao did his job differently from all the municipal commissioners before him and transformed it to make it India's second cleanest city in twenty months flat! All he asked himself was: 'How do I make a *delta*

> You can change your life, your job, your organization, your industry, even your city or country. You can change the world with whatever you are doing right now! There's no such thing as a 'small' job or a 'small' role or 'small' responsibilities. Any job contains within it the potential to change civilization if it is reframed appropriately.

change?' With no additional resources, no support, no directive handed to him, he went about his 'job' and shifted the orbit of an entire city.

SHIFTING THE ORBIT OF AN ENTIRE CITY

When S.R. Rao took charge as Surat's municipal commissioner in May 1995, he inherited a 400-year-old city that had been afflicted by a disease of the middle ages: plague.

Monsoon floods and the filth in Surat's waterlogged streets reportedly caused the plague of Surat in September 1994. In the couple of months following the plague, there was a flurry of activity in Surat and its municipality. But within three months after the plague, it was back to business as usual. Surat was back to being, as an INTACH survey in November 1994 put it, one of the filthiest cities in India. Half of the malarial deaths in Gujarat came from Surat alone. Its open sewers and filthy streets were a disaster waiting to happen. And in 1995, with the monsoon approaching again, the stage seemed set for history to repeat itself.

But then Rao walked in. Legend has it that one morning in May, he sauntered into the municipality office, leaned against a door, took out a tobacco pouch, rolled his trademark cigarette, put it in his mouth, lit it, and introduced himself: 'My name is Rao … S.R. Rao.'

Within two years of Rao taking over, INTACH rated Surat as India's second cleanest city behind Chandigarh. Malaria cases in Surat came down from 22,000 in 1994 to 496 in 1997. The Surat Medical Association reported a decrease of 66 per cent in doctors' earnings as public health measurably improved through better sanitation and with incidences of waterborne diseases crashing.

The population covered by sanitation increased from 63 per cent to 97 per cent. The population covered by protected drinking water increased from 60 per cent to 95 per cent. Clearing of garbage daily went up to 98 per cent from the earlier 40 per cent. Not just this, 92 km of main roads were widened, 300 km of new roads were laid, and the percentage of streets with lighting went up to 98.2.

All within twenty months of Rao taking charge. And the impact continues to this day more than ten years later. For instance, since at least 2002, there have been no malarial deaths at all according to Surat municipality figures. From twenty-two thousand to zero!

Imagine the scale of Rao's achievement. In just twenty months he radically transformed a city. And Surat is no puny town. It is the second largest city in Gujarat after Ahmedabad. It is India's twelfth largest city and with a population of nearly three million, one of the eleven metropolitan cities in India. It has got a population density in some areas of an astounding 54,000 people per square km. Before 1995, over 40 per cent of its population lived in slums, most with no drainage whatsoever. Dirty water flowed and stagnated around houses particularly in the monsoon, with low-lying areas inundated. The city had always been noted for epidemics of waterborne diseases like malaria, gastroenteritis, cholera, dengue and hepatitis. The plague was no accident. It was a logical next step in the disease hierarchy of Surat. Further, the Surat municipality is the oldest in the country and was infested with a corrupt, cynical bureaucracy. And this is the city that Rao transformed in an impossible period of time! It just brings home how much can be done if someone just puts himself behind a cause. For Rao, the cause was clear: eliminate plague and transform Surat.

How did S.R. Rao overcome impossible odds to achieve all this?

According to him, he first challenged the existing myths under which civil servants (or any of us) hide their incompetence:

(i) Existing rules, regulations, hierarchical systems are outmoded and therefore we can't function effectively;

(ii) We have insufficient finances and therefore cannot implement anything effectively;

(iii) We have insufficient and/or unskilled manpower;

(iv) Political and/or administrative interference constantly inhibits our effectiveness; and

(v) There is insufficient delegation of powers. Therefore we have little authority.

While Rao talks about bureaucrats hiding under these myths, these are myths that all of us use as excuses for doing an ordinary job; for not making that attempt to change civilization. We are always going to have insufficient finances, we are always going to have rules and regulations, we are always going to have insufficient/unskilled manpower, we are always going to have political interference and we are rarely going to have enough power. So what's *your* excuse? Are you going to continue cribbing and complaining and living under comforting myths, or are you going to begin making a difference? When you look back at your life, will you see excuses or will you see solid achievements?

When Rao took charge as municipal commissioner of Surat, he was a rookie when it came to municipalities. An IAS officer, he had no previous experience in running a municipality. When he asked his colleagues what could be done about the city, they said, 'Nothing can be done. The people are bad; the citizens are bad. They throw garbage on the streets. We clear the garbage at nine a.m. and it's back at ten. It's part of the genetic make-up of the population here.'

Next, he asked them what he should do. They said that since he was the boss, he had to read all the files and make decisions. And as S.R. Rao says, 'Each day I was getting 500 files. There was no difference between a lowly paid clerk and myself. I was getting thrice the salary, but doing essential the same job. Whatever the clerk started, the entire file would come to me at the end of the day, huge thick ones. In fact, I lost my eyesight. After some time, I stopped reading the files altogether. It did not make any sense.'

After that, he spent his first month just observing what was happening around him. He held meetings, he spoke to people,

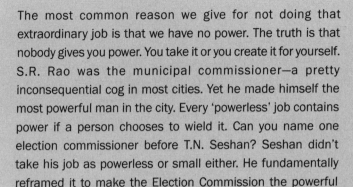

The most common reason we give for not doing that extraordinary job is that we have no power. The truth is that nobody gives you power. You take it or you create it for yourself. S.R. Rao was the municipal commissioner—a pretty inconsequential cog in most cities. Yet he made himself the most powerful man in the city. Every 'powerless' job contains power if a person chooses to wield it. Can you name one election commissioner before T.N. Seshan? Seshan didn't take his job as powerless or small either. He fundamentally reframed it to make the Election Commission the powerful body it is today.

he went to the field. He walked all around Surat. Ten years later, his awed colleagues still talk about how Rao covered every inch of Surat on foot.

With that one month of observation, he had identified the fundamental issues behind Surat's problems. And rather than attack the symptoms of the problems, Rao drilled down to the core issues affecting the municipality and its functioning. First, Rao identified the following symptoms:

(i) Turfism and compartmentalization, with each functionary operating like a mini Turk;

(ii) Knowledge hoarding; because knowledge was power, it wasn't being shared;

(iii) Organizational politics and wars;

(iv) Centralization of powers with no delegation of responsibilities;

(v) Schisms between 'core' functions and 'non-core' ones;

(vi) Treating symptoms in a knee-jerk reaction instead of treating the fundamental disease;

(vii) No 'rule of law'. Everybody operated on personal contacts; and

(viii) A master versus slave mindset that treated the conservancy workers very badly.

From these symptoms, Rao identified three key areas he needed to address at a fundamental level: Administrative Capacity Building, Financial Capacity Building and Public Health Engineering Capacity Building. When Rao addressed these key areas at a core level, civilization, as they knew it, changed for Surat's residents.

In the vast majority of cases, and especially if the problem is large, we tend to tinker around with the symptom. Even if we understand the fundamental cause, often the scale of the challenge intimidates us and we would rather operate at the peripheries. Soon, we find that it needs more and more effort to suppress the symptom and eventually, all our energies and resources go into that suppression and before long, we reach a point of rapidly diminishing returns. We find we need to keep pouring in resources and effort just to stay afloat. For example, stray cattle on the streets were a recurring problem of Surat. The usual solution was to embark on cattle collection drives, pick up cattle from the streets, and deposit them on the outskirts of the city. But they soon found their way back. One day, Rao decided to follow them on foot to see where they went, what they did. He found that they went from one garbage bin to another on the streets. Therefore, instead of clearing the cattle, he broke down the garbage bins and collected garbage from homes directly and dumped the garbage on the outskirts. The cattle followed. Surat has been cattle-free since.

ADMINISTRATIVE CAPACITY BUILDING

Rao worked on each of his three key areas almost simultaneously, but the first step was to set his internal house in order. And he did that with administrative capacity building. Rao knew that in order to hold his people accountable for results, he first had to provide them with responsibility, with the authority and freedom to make decisions that goes along with responsibility. In many cases, we hand down responsibility, but not the authority to make decisions. And this effectively ties people's hands.

To provide authority, Rao made all functional heads commissioners. Overnight, Surat had eleven commissioners with the same administrative and financial powers of the erstwhile commissioner. Surat was also divided into six zones and each zone was given to a commissioner to handle as a mini-corporation. The main objective of this was to end compartmentalization which is the bane of bureaucracy. Each of his subordinates would otherwise have headed different departments and created vertical turf-protecting hierarchies. To eliminate this Rao made them handle geographical regions instead. And to ensure effectiveness, he devolved both administrative and financial powers to them and held them accountable for their regions, demanding detailed work plans, road maps and clear tangible results in key areas. All the powers of the municipal commissioner were devolved to the new commissioners, including financial powers to allocate up to Rs 200,000 per project without prior approval. This was empowerment in its truest sense.

Rao disbanded functional departments. Earlier there was a chief engineer, roads, who would not cooperate with a chief engineer, sewerage, who would not cooperate with the chief engineer, water, and so on. Rao decided they did not need functional departments. Their services were outsourced to private companies that were

We often pay lip service to empowerment by making a person responsible for certain outcomes, but then require that person to check back with us for every minor (or major) decision. It's great to feel 'in control', to say yes or no, to be wanted, needed, sought after. And it can be extremely frightening to give up this security blanket. But do you really have a choice? Orbit shifters like Rao don't so much 'empower' as create opportunities for people to perform on their own. Many organizations pay lip service to 'independent' 'stand-alone' businesses and products. But they all route through a single sales force, have a single buying/purchasing department, HR, etc. And they call themselves independent! How are you ever going to get accountability from business heads if they are always tied to other departments' strings? Independence means entrepreneurship. Which means they need to run their own operations end to end. If Rao could create entrepreneurship in a huge bureaucracy, what's stopping you?

held accountable. The chief engineers were made commissioners for particular areas and they handled everything end-to-end: taxation, personnel, sanitation, water and sewerage. This brought departmental walls and barriers crashing down.

Rao held daily review meetings with his entire top team. They met to discuss the day's happenings and also to plan for the next day's requirements. All decisions were made jointly, including allocation of resources.

Rao also introduced a time-based citizen complaint redressal system and tracked it online. He made a list of complaints that should be addressed within twenty-four hours, those to be addressed within forty-eight hours, those within three days and finally some engineering works that needed to be addressed

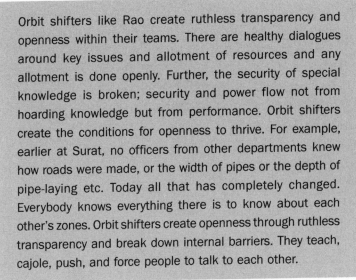

Orbit shifters like Rao create ruthless transparency and openness within their teams. There are healthy dialogues around key issues and allotment of resources and any allotment is done openly. Further, the security of special knowledge is broken; security and power flow not from hoarding knowledge but from performance. Orbit shifters create the conditions for openness to thrive. For example, earlier at Surat, no officers from other departments knew how roads were made, or the width of pipes or the depth of pipe-laying etc. Today all that has completely changed. Everybody knows everything there is to know about each other's zones. Orbit shifters create openness through ruthless transparency and break down internal barriers. They teach, cajole, push, and force people to talk to each other.

within seven days. And he tracked these complaints every day at the daily reviews. Citizens were given Rao's number to contact if a job was marked as done and not really done or if the job wasn't done in the stipulated time. This ruthless transparency soon created a high performing group that began to work together as a real team because they all faced similar problems and needed help from each other.

According to the Surat Municipal Corporation, between September 1995 and December 1996, over 90,000 complaints had been received, all of which had been addressed within the stipulated timeframe! That's what brutal transparency does.

Orbit shifters make it a point to experience first-hand the conditions their 'customers' operate in. Without first-hand experience, everything else is assumption and rationalization. To ensure this happened, Rao created the AC to DC rule (from Air Conditioned offices to Daily Chores on the field). All

How open is your organization? Sooner or later, all organizations become vertical; and departmental loyalties transcend organizational effectiveness. We almost instinctively form in-groups and out-groups. The only way to break free of this is to create total transparency. If you need to make a fundamental transformation happen in your team, you are going to need ruthless transparency. Which means constantly battling the departmental walls that keep popping up like mushrooms. What are you going to do about it? When are you going to begin?

commissioners would spend compulsorily at least five hours a day in the field. From 7 a.m. to 3 p.m. was field time—all 365 days of the year. Half of this time was to be spent in supervising the slums. Every day till 3 p.m. no AC was permitted to run in any office. Rao himself would be on the field. And if he didn't find an officer on the field, sparks would fly.

Initially, there was a lot of resistance to this with the commissioners saying that they needed to be in the office to meet people who came to see them. Rao replied that people came to see them (usually with complaints) because they weren't doing their job properly. If they did their job well, people wouldn't need to come to the municipality offices. So they would really be far more effective on the field than in the office. And once the junior staff saw their bosses become result oriented, submitting to discipline and being held accountable, they had no objection when their bosses demanded the same of them.

Very soon, as officers experienced first-hand the conditions different citizen groups lived under (at times the officers had to wade through chest-high sewage water), rapid changes began to take place.

——◆——

How often do you actually leave your office and meet the person you are supposed to be serving—the end customer? It doesn't matter what department you work in. Unless you engage with the customer's world, you can't make a dent in your own work. When you are on the field, problems and issues become real. They are no more abstractions. When you look at a piece of paper, all you get is a representation of the problem. You don't experience reality. And if you don't experience reality, you can't begin to make a difference. When you get a piece of paper outlining the problem, it's easier to treat the symptom. When you go on the field, you begin to recognize and treat the disease.

——◆——

Rao also focused on the twin principles of discipline and reward: discipline from the top, reward from the bottom. Rao decided that it was no use targeting the lowest rungs first when it came to disciplining the system. This is often done and it is the easiest way out but not very effective. To be effective, discipline must be imposed top down. When people lower down see that the top exercises discipline and follows (or are made to follow) the rules laid down, they voluntarily follow rules themselves.

All discipline was first imposed at the top. His immediate reportees were made accountable through the AC to DC rule, through daily meetings, and later, through strictly monitored time-based redressal of citizen complaints. At the bottom, the conservancy workers were recognized and rewarded for good work. Their photos were published in newspapers. Also, since the conservancy workers lived in the dirtiest parts of the city where

In most cases we find organizations doing the reverse. They give benefits and perks to the top and regulate or punish from the bottom. The powerless are usually the most affected, getting all the brickbats and a far smaller share of the rewards. This just breeds cynicism and a sense of unfairness. How would your organization be different if you began following Rao's principles?

little or no sanitation reached, Rao decided to clean up these parts first so that they could experience for themselves what it was like to live under clean, hygienic conditions.

Consistent applications of these measures resulted in highly effective micro planning and rationalization (as Rao calls it). Before Rao introduced his measures, like any other governmental body, the SMC was ruled by the most powerful. Any subordinate officer who had political clout could manipulate resources—human, material, machine and finance. These resources are key to the efficacy of municipal services. And if they don't reach the areas that need them the most, disasters happen. As these measures took hold, strict norms were set for resource allocation: the worst affected areas would get priority in terms of resources and focused attention. The results of this micro planning were stupendous. As Rao says, pre May 1995 the level of sanitation was 35 per cent, solid waste removal was 40 per cent. Post micro planning and with just 10 per cent of additional investment, 95 per cent of Surat is covered by daily sanitation, and 97 per cent of solid waste is lifted every day.

Once he had begun the process of setting his internal house in order, Rao embarked on imposing 'moral authority' (as he called it) on the citizens of Surat.

First was the process of education. Eateries were given individual cleanliness instructions. While municipal sweepers were to collect garbage from house to house in a trolley and transport it to the nearest municipal garbage collection point, all commercial establishments including shops and roadside eating joints were instructed to maintain a dustbin in front of their shops and to ensure that cleanliness was maintained in the vicinity. Restaurants and hotels were instructed to maintain bins for collecting refuse and they also had to pack and dispose the garbage at designated sites. Field employees would train and inform housewives on how to sort, pack and dispose garbage. In slum localities regular programmes were conducted to disseminate knowledge on cleanliness and hygiene.

After three months, there was some improvement, but not enough. Citizens continued to throw garbage on the streets and the commissioners were getting disheartened. To create a delta change in the situation, Rao decided to enforce the regulatory aspect of the SMC's role. Here again he followed his 'discipline begins from the top and rewards from the bottom' rule. In this case, it was regulation enforcement from the top and development work from the bottom. He launched what he called the Surat First campaign to recreate Surat. He began punishing the city's most powerful individuals while simultaneously focusing on slum cleanliness, sewage, water and sanitation services.

To enforce discipline, Rao took immediate action in three areas: illegal construction, poor hygiene standards, and property tax evasion. He demolished an illegal building of the most powerful and politically connected man in Surat. Simultaneously, he raided the city's most prestigious and powerful five-star hotel that wasn't complying with regulations. He also attached the property of Surat's biggest defaulter—a mafia don. In one swoop he attacked the powerful vested interests rather than go after the powerless. Imposition of moral authority had begun. For ten days he didn't take any phone calls or respond to messages while he went hammer and tongs after the powerful, demolishing, raiding and attaching property.

Once he began the process of imposing moral authority, Rao removed all escape buttons. To ensure that no external pressures would interrupt him, he refused to take any calls or messages and began operating from the field so that he couldn't be met at the office. Transformations begin with a bang and then peter out because escape buttons aren't removed. Powerful vested interests will always exert more than their fair share of pressure to reverse all such initiatives. Any large-scale transformation you envisage will need to take into account these pressures and reflect on how to neutralize them. In Rao's case, he tided over the first swell of resistance by refusing to be available for private discussions while he went about enforcing his change. He was available only on very public platforms that created huge transparency and neutralized resistors. Later he used public support from the press, the citizens and the judiciary to overcome resistance.

Legend has it that he did something else. He gave all his staff walkie-talkies and insisted on being reached himself only by walkie-talkie. And all walkie-talkie communications were official, therefore recorded. Whenever anyone called him on the walkie-talkie to pressurize him, Rao increased the volume of the walkie-talkie so that all the people around him—press, citizens, staff etc—could hear what was being said and who was trying to exert pressure on him to roll back. This amazing transparency soon ensured that the number of people exerting overt pressure reduced dramatically as they found themselves exposed publicly.

He simultaneously set his internal house in order by forcing the resignations of six first and second rung officers. For those who refused to resign, taking a leaf out of *The Godfather*, Rao says he made them an offer they couldn't refuse. I'll leave it to the reader's imagination what the offers were. He took disciplinary action against 1200 employees ranging from sweepers to officers. This sent a very clear message that non-performance would not be tolerated and those who didn't want to change and insisted on blocking development work would be dealt with harshly.

The internal and external imposition of moral authority began swaying the public towards cooperating with Rao. The press

What Rao did was to use antecedents and consequences. Antecedents are the triggers and structures that make it easy to do the right thing. Consequences reward people for doing the right thing. At Surat, those who persisted in doing wrong were 'made offers they couldn't refuse'. How do *you* motivate people? In our experience, most people are very good at creating antecedents but awfully poor at creating sustained consequences.

supported him; the judiciary supported him with the chief justice even putting a stop to stay orders that would have prevented Rao from carrying out his demolitions. Rao imposed a fine on those who chucked garbage on the roads. When he was reminded that he had no authority to impose fines, he levied 'administrative charges' on the grounds that he would have to clean the roads an extra time because of people littering roads with garbage.

The introduction of administrative charges began a sea change in citizens' habits. It also increased social vigilance at the community level. People participated in the entire exercise not merely by disposing their own refuse in garbage bins but also by ensuring that no one threw garbage on the streets or in front of one's house. The result: clean roads and neighbourhoods. Even the area around every garbage bin is spotlessly clean.

The impact of the Surat First campaign and operation Moral Authority was that once citizens saw that the rule of law was really equal for everyone, they began taking a real pride in their city. Many came forward to voluntarily demolish their own illegal structures. As Rao says, he widened 200 km of roads that were under stay orders. This could only be done because many people voluntarily gave their property for widening roads.

FINANCIAL CAPACITY BUILDING

In parallel with administrative capacity building, Rao worked on financial capacity building. To bring about the changes Rao envisaged would cost money. And the corporators had flatly refused to increase taxes to help these changes. If Rao needed money, he would have to find it himself.

To build financial capacity, he did four major things:

(i)   Plugged loopholes in property taxation;
(ii)   Plugged loopholes in octroi collections;
(iii) Computerized accounts and brought in commercial accounting norms as against government accounting norms; and
(iv)   Adopted a profit centre approach to bring in efficiencies in service delivery. Each zone was an independent profit centre that generated its own revenues and had to deliver effective service.

Property tax assessment was being done once in four years for a short period and all municipal employees were roped in for this period to assess property, under the guidance of those in the property taxation department. This led to a lot of irregularities because those in the department could be bribed to undervalue the property and they would get this okayed by the part-time employees. Later, if there was an enquiry, the property tax authorities could always say that a part-time worker from another department did the assessment and therefore he may have made a mistake.

To plug this loophole and to increase accountability, Rao decided to use only full-time property tax employees, and get them to assess property tax every year, but over a year rather than a one-month burst. However, the corporators refused to let him assess every year. Assessment could only be done once in four years, they insisted. To overcome this handicap, Rao divided the city into four zones and got the employees to assess tax over a full year in each zone. This ensured an annual tax inflow, as well as increased accountability and still allowed for the corporators' condition of assessment once in four years.

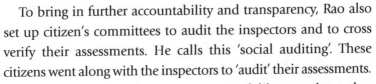

Your ability to succeed at an orbit-shifting mission is directly linked to your ability to tolerate frustration. Rao faced hostile politicians who kept trying to undercut him. They refused to let him fine citizens for littering, they refused to increase taxes, though by now most citizens were okay with that; they refused to let him collect property tax annually. At every step he was blocked. And he always found a way around the blocks. Every obstacle was combated with an innovation that found a way around the rules. How much frustration can *you* tolerate?

To bring in further accountability and transparency, Rao also set up citizen's committees to audit the inspectors and to cross verify their assessments. He calls this 'social auditing'. These citizens went along with the inspectors to 'audit' their assessments. This brought in brutal transparency. And like anywhere else, when transparency came in effectiveness followed.

Octroi collections had leakages that Rao was determined to plug. He set up flying squads to monitor check-posts and also introduced walkie-talkies and closed loop wireless communication between check-posts and the centre to ensure that no truck escaped the net. Again, social auditing was used here as a cross-verification mechanism.

The results were stunning:

(i)   97 per cent of property tax arrears collected (of arrears totalling Rs 102 crores);

(ii)   Unassessed properties yielding annually Rs 30 crores in taxes brought into the net;

(iii)   Under-assessed properties yielding annually Rs 18 crores in taxes brought into net;

(iv)   Property tax collection efficiency increased from 30 per cent to over 80 per cent;

(v)   Octroi collections jumped 19 per cent.

The net effect was an astounding 54 per cent increase in revenue income for the year 1995–96 over the previous year. The revenue income in 1994–95 was Rs 164.7 crores. In 1995–96 it was Rs 253 crores!

Capacity Building in Public Health Engineering

Both administrative and financial capacity building were aimed at improving public health. After all, this was the city of the plague.

One of the first things that Rao did was to break the stranglehold of a cartel of eighteen contractors who ensured that any tenders that were floated for maintenance jobs always went to them. They fixed prices and prevented other contractors from submitting proposals or blocked their proposals.

Rao decided to break this cartel and end the lack of transparency in the system. To do this, he fixed a unit rate for each contract annually. For example, if maintenance required 5000 tube lights to be replaced annually, he fixed a unit price for each tube light valid for a year and contractors were invited to apply for the annual contract to supply tube lights at that rate. In one stroke, he ended up creating 300 new contractors. Transparency again!

Also, so far, according to government rules, every time tenders were floated, advertisements were required in a minimum of four newspapers. These led to huge advertising costs. With his unit rate system that signed contractors on for annual contracts, these costs crashed.

For long-term or 'once through' projects, he brought in a '6 month–6 page' rule. Most government departments have a standard eighteen-month period of project completion no matter how simple or complex the project. As Rao says, since he's not an engineer, he doesn't understand an engineer's constraints and therefore brought in the 6 month–6 page rule. A chief engineer had to complete a project in six months—after all, he argued, if all projects could be done in eighteen months, they could be done in six months too. If the chief engineer believed it could not be done in six months he had to write a document of not less than six pages, single spaced, explaining why it couldn't be done. Most engineers found it easier to finish the project in six months rather than explain in such detail and depth why it couldn't be done.

Rao also brought about considerable changes in slum living conditions. He persuaded them to break down encroachments so that he could build new roads into the slums, along with increasing public toilets and piped water supply.

To extend sewerage and drainage facilities in congested slums, where inner lanes were often barely three feet wide, Rao needed the consent of the slum dwellers to demolish some parts of their houses. The slum dwellers, in most cases, not only agreed but also came forward to sacrifice parts of their land and dwelling for the common good. In many cases they themselves demolished parts of their huts in order to facilitate the SMC project of widening of inner lanes for carrying the service lines. In one slum, the inner lanes have been widened to almost ten feet. The open drains that used to carry both sewage and storm water have been laid under the ground. The people there are now very happy as there has been no water logging in recent monsoons, whereas before the renovation, the area used to be under as much as six feet of water during the rainy season. As a consequence, the incidence of waterborne diseases has also declined considerably. The net result was that over 82 per cent of slums had been upgraded by the time Rao left Surat.

SUSTAINING THE CHANGE

Rao was in Surat for just twenty months before he was transferred. Yet his systems and results have continued more than a decade later. The only major flooding after Rao left happened in 2006, when one of the dams on the Narmada was suddenly opened during a heavy monsoon downpour. And Rao was again dispatched to Surat to deal with the flooding. And as Amarjit Singh, commissioner of health, Gujarat, put it, Rao instantly brought order back to the city on a war footing. What has caused this amazing sustainability?

Five factors have contributed to Rao's work enduring after him:

One, it is very difficult to reverse a good system. As Rao says, 'When I show people what is possible, they won't be satisfied with less later. If they never see what is possible, what can be done, they never dream and never have any expectations. Today because this has worked, everyone, from the politicians to the municipal body, is now measured on this parameter.'

Two, sustainability requires sacrifices. But you can't expect people to sacrifice without giving something back in return. For every take away, give something to compensate. In this case, it was civic pride and the pleasure of seeing a truly clean city.

Three, sacrifices come from ownership and when people perceive that the law is equal for everyone. When I realize that the rule of law is truly equal, even if I believe that I may lose something, if it's fair, I don't mind. When people see a very clear rule of law, they begin to cooperate and make sacrifices. For example, as Rao says, 'Widening roads was not possible because the property could not be purchased, as a stay order was taken from the courts. And yet people pulled down their own structures. I couldn't do it because of the stay order. They could do it and they did it. The sacrifice this entailed was considerable. In Surat, property prices are 70 per cent black and 30 per cent white. I could pay them only the 30 per cent. They willingly let go of the 70.'

Four, sustainability also comes when the environment is clean. When something is spotless, we don't willingly sully it. When it is dirty anyway, we don't mind adding to it. This is true of the physical environment as well as the ethical.

Five, sustainability comes from social auditing. From getting citizens involved in the regulatory and developmental aspects of governance. Mahila mandals, youth clubs and other associations were involved in social auditing. They were told to report if they came across something that was not satisfactory. Rao also brought in time-bound tasks and an appellate body to approach in case of lapses. With social auditing, citizens not only audited the municipal commission but also each other.

To give an idea as to why Surat has sustained what Rao began, here is what the Surat web site says about the steps taken to control malaria and filaria. Along with active surveillance work, the surveillance workers also impart health education among the public for prevention of vector-borne diseases. School health programmes, street meetings and meetings amongst members of mahila mandals, Anganwadi, and NGOs are organized to impart knowledge of malaria. The menace of mosquitoes and how to fight it is demonstrated in school puppet shows. Street plays are performed in slum areas and local dailies display prominent advertisements during the anti-malaria month. Live debates on malaria are organized in the local TV channels. Anyone whose house is detected as a breeding ground for mosquitoes is promptly prosecuted. A total of 1821 complaints were filed before the court during the year under report and the court imposed fines totalling Rs 118,110 on offenders. Administrative charges of Rs 945,165 were recovered from defaulters whose carelessness abetted the breeding of mosquitoes.

S.R. Rao, the Person

What really stands out in conversations with Rao is his emphasis on 'character building'. He says tough decisions build character. It's always easy to take the easy way out. People will pressure you, threaten you. There are always pressures, but every individual needs to have boundary conditions—conditions beyond which he will not bend.

His refuses to let the system overpower him. As he says, mega-myths exist about the helplessness of the bureaucracy. A civil servant has more than enough power and ways to overcome hurdles if he chooses to do so. Instead of complaining about the lack of resources and wasting his time over what he couldn't control, Rao focused on what he could control and used that to make a difference.

Rao has a keen ability to cut through the clutter and think through the solution. He joined as a first-time municipal

> What stands out in orbit shifters like Rao is that they always find ways to overcome obstacles. Ways always exist. It's just that the vast majority of us don't bother to exercise the six inches between our ears. It's far easier to go along and not buck the tide. But the price for that is boring mediocrity—and possibly being one of the first to be laid off in any downsizing.

commissioner, knew nothing about the system, learnt for a month, identified the loopholes, put a plan in place and followed it through with almost fanatical zeal.

He refuses to let adversity get the better of him. His work was hampered by the corporate councillors at all stages, and when he was carrying out the demolitions of the illegal constructions of the rich and powerful, he was threatened, his wife received obscene phone calls, his son was kidnapped and went missing for forty-eight hours, but he held firm.

He has the uncanny ability to get the citizens of the city rooting for him and even demolishing their illegal constructions on their own. He imbued the city with civic pride. He is clear that when discipline is enforced top down and rewards are given bottom up, delta changes take place. Above all, he constantly questions himself and others: have you made a delta change today?

Orbit-shifting transformations happened when Rao asked himself a single question ... everyday. Ask yourself the same question: have you made a *delta change* today? If you haven't yet, what are you going to do about it?

Rao has moved from strength to strength. After Surat, he was deputed to the centre and took over the Visakhapatnam Port Trust. He made it the most effective in the country on almost all parameters. After that, Chandrababu Naidu, then chief minister of Andhra Pradesh, requested him for a special deputation to the Hyderabad municipality. The increase in road width as well as the cleanliness and road quality in Hyderabad today are directly attributed to him. After another stint in Gujarat, today he is in New Delhi as the additional secretary, department of information and technology.

12

SU-KAM

CREATING AN INDUSTRY

A question many budding entrepreneurs ask themselves is: How do I create a new business? The smarter among them ask: What does it take to create an industry?

Su-Kam and its founder managing director Kunwer Sachdev are a textbook example of what it takes to create not just a business, but an industry. Beginning with nothing more than an idea and Rs 10,000 as capital, today Su-Kam is the biggest Indian corporate in the power backup industry. Last year they had revenues of around Rs 600 crores. They have a presence in more than 50 countries, employ 1200 people across 23 offices, have 6000-plus network partners, and aspire to touch 50,000 network partners or dealers over the next three years. They have more than 50 per cent market share in the organized sector.

So how did Kunwer create an industry where none existed? The first step was of course to spot the opportunity—and it took a different way of perceiving reality to do that. The second was to create a superior product that was clearly differentiated in the market. The third was to create a distribution channel and a brand. The fourth was to emerge with wave after wave of innovation that left the competition gasping—and in the process of creating these waves of innovation, an industry was created. At every step, what drove success was a continuous focus on non-dilution. Everything taken up had to be the best in the world. As the people at Su-Kam say, their market is not limited to India; it's the global market they are going after.

THE BEGINNING

It all began in 1997 when Kunwer bought an inverter for use at home. The quality was so poor that almost every second day a service person would come over trying to fix its innumerable problems. Since Kunwer had a fair idea about manufacturing electric and electronic systems, being then in the cable TV business and manufacturing parts for cable operators, he decided to open the inverter himself. Though he doesn't have a technical background, what he saw inside made him decide to take on the inverter business. As he says, 'I opened the inverter and saw that it could not function the way it was currently made. So the industry couldn't grow because if a product doesn't work there's no way the industry can grow.'

He saw this as a huge opportunity. Since India is perennially short of power, technically every single household in India could be sold an inverter! Also, Indian power conditions were so bad, no inverter imported from outside could work effectively in India. India needed its own technologically customized inverters that would be able to handle the frequent and extreme fluctuations in power as well as get charged in very erratic power supply conditions. Finally, because the industry was made up of a number of small local players, nobody owned the market. He decided to enter the inverter and power backup industry.

What is amazing is that there were many large players in India in the electrical and consumer durables fields. No one saw an opportunity here. The main block is that many of them identified themselves with their existing products alone. But it isn't too difficult for, say, refrigerator manufacturers to figure out that their refrigerators don't work four to five hours every day in most homes across India. If they had looked at what prevents their refrigerators working, they just might have seen a huge opportunity in the electricity storage and generation business.

The first step in creating and owning a new industry is to identify an area where a number of small mom and pop businesses exist in a category that has huge potential demand. A nascent industry always has a huge number of unorganized players until it begins consolidating. Technology and standards in a nascent industry don't really exist. Think of the computer industry in its infancy. Almost anyone could enter it until consolidation began to happen. A number of organizations create new businesses and new business models by organizing the unorganized and by branding the unbranded. There were dozens of small independent booksellers in India until Landmark and Crosswords happened. Hospitals in India stayed independent family businesses till Dr Prathap Reddy came in and created the Apollo chain of hospitals with consistent standards, and people began to trust the institution and the brand rather than the individual surgeon alone.

Having spotted the opportunity, Kunwer began with a small prototype. Along with the engineers from his cable TV business he studied almost all the inverters available in the Indian market in 1997. They realized that all inverters had the same ineffective

capacitor technology that made them so unreliable. At the time
generators were preferred to inverters because of the unreliability
that caused the inverter battery to run down. The only exception
was Videocon's inverter. But this inverter was suitable more for
the stable power conditions of the developed world. In the West,
power is stable so inverters don't need to cope with a wide range
of fluctuations. Also, most inverters there are used for outdoor
events like long boat rides or for camping when car or boat
batteries are used with inverters to run equipment like TVs or
microwaves or stereo systems. The first inverter launched
successfully by Su-Kam was an improvised version of the
Videocon inverter adapted to Indian power conditions.

Inverters in the West are used more as outdoor aids. As a
result, some of the premier international power solutions
companies already in India for several years either didn't see
the huge opportunity or were unable to convince their principals
abroad about the opportunity space that existed in India. Most
MNCs cannot easily spot an opportunity like this because in
their countries they don't have problems like these. So they
look at markets in other geographies from the lens of existing
markets in their own countries. In the West, inverters are largely
limited to the outdoor leisure activities market. Outdoor leisure
activities don't much exist in India, ergo: no market exists.

When Kunwer launched his first inverter, he knew his current
team of cable TV engineers wouldn't be able to innovate further
or develop new technology—and technology was clearly the route
to take. He would need to hire others. But who should he hire,
and from where? The inverter industry didn't exist as an industry.
There were only a few assemblers around. Hiring them wouldn't

lead to breakthroughs in product technology. So finally, scouring across industries, he put together an eclectic bunch of people. Some were from the UPS industry, some from diverse digital product industries, some even from the missile industry. A company working on components for the Agni missile had wound up and the engineers there had nowhere to go. Kunwer enrolled them.

Today, one of his R&D heads is one of the missile people. His head of production is from the automobile industry. This has enabled the team to look for ideas outside the usual electrical industry best practices. For instance, in production they use an assembly and just in time (JIT) delivery system taken from the auto industry. The missile engineers brought in

Perhaps the first step in the move from small-time to big-time is an interest in growing the technology in parallel with growing the business. The market was always there for inverters. Rather than meet demand at the lowest common denominator by taking a short-term view of the market and supplying what everyone else was supplying, Kunwer made the shift to developing the industry and its technology by employing highly trained professionals. Those who just made fix-it-yourself inverters stayed small scale. Kunwer made the leap by hiring, developing, and growing in-house technological talent. More importantly, he focused on the growth of the industry. Meeting market demand and ensuring the growth of the industry are two very different mindsets and by no means limited to smaller organizations and nascent industries. If your industry isn't quite growing, most key players in the industry may have succumbed to the temptation of 'serving' the market rather than driving it through innovations.

an understanding of components and their performance under extreme conditions.

Once Kunwer decided to drive growth through technology, he sourced the MOSFET technology from abroad and the next inverter they made in 1998 was based on this. MOSFET (Metal Oxide Semiconductor Field-Effect Transistor, a device used to amplify or switch electronic signals) meant that they could reduce the size of the inverter to one-fourth, thereby reducing costs, improving efficiency and enabling them to use one battery instead of two. With the MOSFET inverter, Kunwer and his team created a differentiated, superior product. They had crashed the costs of the inverter, as well as set a reference point of what is possible.

DISTRIBUTION AND BRANDING

When Su-Kam came out with the reliable MOSFET inverter, many local manufacturers were in a dilemma; they could match neither Su-Kam's price nor quality. Kunwer made them an offer they couldn't refuse. He told them that he was going to radically change the technology year on year starting with the MOSFET. They had two choices: either match his innovations to stay in the market, or join him as distributors or dealers. As he says, 'In every city there were dozens of people manufacturing inverters. And there were two kinds of people: manufacturers and battery dealers. I converted the manufacturers into distributors, and the battery guy into dealers, and we created a network.'

Look at the way the industry began to consolidate under Kunwer. The unbundled players began to get bundled and an unbranded, indifferent product began to acquire increasing levels of technology through innovations to drive differentiation and quality.

Building a business from the ground up, where no industry existed wasn't easy. In the move from unorganized industry to organized, there were a lot of challenges. They had to create and train sales and service people from scratch. They had to get people from other industries, train them, inspire them and send them into the field. They began channel meets and dealer meets and began to educate the dealer and distributor about the product attributes. It was a period of great effort but it laid the seeds for a new industry.

Su-Kam needed to build a highly visible brand with minimal advertising expense. Again Kunwer needed to think differently. When he saw that Airtel had put its banners on all possible walls and pillars, he thought of some place which had not been targeted by anyone. In 2000, Kunwer was the first person to put up banners of Su-Kam on almost every single dhaba or tea shop that lined the length of all major highways. This gave Su-Kam immediate visibility. But the challenge was that the shop owners would remove the hoardings sooner or later as the boards were not important to them. Kunwer came up with a win-win proposition. He put the names of the dhabas too on the banner/board so that not only did Su-Kam get publicity, but the individual dhaba owners got it as well. He reiterates that he is the first person to start this at this scale and it has now become fairly common, but he got tremendous mileage out of it.

Su-Kam was also the first in the power backup industry in India to start strip advertising in the classified columns to save costs. He'd take up nearly half a page of classifieds and make a large 'Su-Kam' out of it as a half-page of classifieds was much cheaper than buying a regular half-page ad. He then moved on to colour and electronic media advertisements. As he says, many newspapers changed their classifieds policies because of him. Advertisements were placed in newspapers until Su-Kam became a household name known for brilliant technology and dependable products.

THE PRODUCT INNOVATIONS

With the brand building and channel development, product innovations were going on simultaneously. Su-Kam launched a new innovation almost every year. As Kunwer says, 'I change my whole product within a year. The moment the current product is ready I start working on a fundamentally different second product.' And does he systematically kill the product after three to four years? 'I try to kill it, sometimes it is killed itself. Even if my earlier product is more successful that the current one, I see to it that it is not manufactured after a couple of years, irrespective of whether the market kills it or not. Why?

Contrast this with the hawk-eyed manner in which most brand and category managers watch out for cannibalization. *Their* bread and butter, not the organization's, depends on cannibalization not happening and they do everything they can to prevent it. We love Peter Drucker's question in this context: 'What are you going to systematically abandon in the next three years?' Many organizations fall in love with their successful products and spend a lot of time and effort in polishing and improving them and focusing on them to the extent that they stop focusing on creating the next big thing. Sure they go about working on new ideas, but not the way they would if their current cash cow were going off the market in the next couple of years. Drucker's question advocates systematic abandonment so that you are forced to create new breakthroughs before the market shifts catch you unawares.

Because I want to drive the market—I don't want to be driven by it. In every case people who became leaders never thought of changing and when change came in from the outside, they were stuck. My guiding principle is: change the market before it changes you.'

Su-Kam is the only organization in the industry with an R&D unit certified by the Department of Scientific and Industrial Research (DSIR), Government of India. The R&D facility at Su-Kam has state-of-the-art equipment for testing and developing products.

Kunwer's attitude towards the market is one of constant movement. As one of the members of the R&D team put it, 'Whatever we launch anybody will copy it, or will arrive at that platform in the next two to three years.' Hence, the underlying philosophy at Su-Kam, in the words of another R&D employee is, 'Regular production should be there but focus should be on next couple of years. What we have developed will continue for the next three years, but after that the product will be obsolete. So you have to be ready with the product for the next three years. And then on to the next three years.'

As you can see, Kunwer's attitude has permeated the organization. What more could a leader ask for?

The challenge that Su-Kam faces is that its output is not clearly visible to the end consumer. Su-Kam's constant focus is to provide purer and purer power. It has become a passion to provide the best quality of power of possible. As Su-Kam's director of operations, Naresh Kaushik, says, 'Today you don't know on what kind of power supply your fridge and TV are running. And maybe equipment that should have run for six years without breaking down is running only for three years and you are still happy. It's a happiness born out of an ignorance of what is possible. When you put an inverter in your house you don't know how much electricity it uses. For example, it gives you backup for four hours, but to have that backup you never know how much electricity it has taken from the main supply. Maybe it has taken for ten hours and since you don't know how your electricity bill is rising, you are content.'

Innovation at Su-Kam, then, has been a constant search to add value through driving technology as well as to find a way to differentiate externally for the consumer. It has come out with innovations almost every year to drive value as well as differentiation.

After the MOSFET inverter in 1998, in 2001, Kunwer launched India's first sine wave technology inverter. The existing technology then was the more primitive square wave. Sine wave gives a pure form of power that can run sensitive appliances. This technology wasn't new to the world, but Indian power conditions have inconsistent surges and huge voltage fluctuations. Hence, using sine wave here required customizing the technology to suit India. But how do you even begin testing it without a lab? Kunwer and his team identified two extreme conditions and places to test and develop the technology for India. Meerut and Kanpur had the dubious honour of being the two places in India where any inverter would consistently fail, thanks to rampant power fluctuations. These became his live laboratories. The technology was developed and tested till finally, a successful inverter was made that not only eliminated the irritating humming sound that inverters made but also transformed the quality of the power produced.

THE PLASTIC BODY INVERTERS

Launched in 2002, the plastic body inverters were not just unique in India, but also in the world. All inverters at the time were made of metal, because the temperature on usage would go up to 120 degrees and there was no other material that could withstand such high temperatures. He knew that using plastic would make an inverter visually appealing, lighter in weight and shockproof as well. So what Kunwer had to do was find a plastic that would not melt. He found his answer with GE Plastics. They developed a plastic for him that was stable at high temperatures. And suddenly the customer had a range of lightweight, attractive inverters to choose from.

When Kunwer approached GE, he went not only with a working model of the inverter but also with a mould pre-designed by another Indian manufacturer. GE had only to supply the right kind of plastic. With that was made the world's first plastic-body inverter. There were of course voices of doubt. How could an inverter be made of plastic? The industry thought Kunwer had lost it. But the market and customers loved it. It was a hit. So, as usual, the competition began copying it. But they copied what they saw, not what went behind the making of the Su-Kam inverter—the intense testing and the backing of a large reputed material supplier. The competition began making inverters with plastic, and the inevitable happened: they started melting. Complaints began pouring in and the governments of UP and Punjab intervened to test the plastic-body inverters of all companies. Only one company cleared the tests and was allowed to continue manufacturing plastic inverters: Su-Kam.

THE HOME UPS

In 2003 came the next success for Su-Kam, when Kunwer decided to integrate two separate power backup devices, the inverter and the UPS, to make, as he says, the first-in-the-world 'Home UPS'. Such an integration would help in two ways:

1. If a UPS was to work as an inverter, the power backup duration would grow exponentially—from 10–15 minutes to 2–3 hours!

2. If an inverter was to work as a UPS, the power produced would be consistent and even more pure than the one provided by the grid. In addition, the switchover time (time taken by the power backup device to switch on after the power goes off) would reduce from 50–100 milliseconds to 0–5 milliseconds. This would be good for every single electrical equipment in the house.

Once Kunwer thought of this path-breaking idea, it was only a matter of time before India and the world saw the first-ever 'Home UPS' system, thanks to Su-Kam's consistent R&D and numerous innovations. But as with the plastic-body inverters, the competitors began criticizing this. 'How could an inverter be a home UPS?' But Kunwer had studied the definitions closely. If the switchover time was less than ten milliseconds, a product would qualify as a UPS.

There were tremendous benefits too. A UPS was taxed at 4 per cent, while an inverter was taxed at 12 per cent. By creating a home UPS, Kunwer came under the 4 per cent bracket. Something he leveraged to cut the prices of his product further.

Again the inevitable happened. The entire industry tried to copy the product to reap the tax benefits, but as before, they didn't bother to do what Kunwer had done: reduce the switchover time. They just began branding their inverters as home UPS. The government got suspicious and got the products tested. Again all but Su-Kam failed.

In 2005, Su-Kam launched the high-frequency sine wave inverter. Something that has further shrunk the size of the inverter and provides a very high quality of pure power.

It is almost as if Kunwer was playing with the competition. Putting in products without explaining what truly differentiated them and then letting the competition shoot themselves in their collective feet when they began copying. Clearly, it's the approach, not of a small-time business, but of a technology leader who constantly seeks to upgrade and bring in new-to-the-world innovations. The interesting thing is that Kunwer made others, including MNCs in the inverter industry, look like small-towners when they began copying his innovations without understanding what went behind them.

In 2008, the 250 VA inverter that can run one tube light and a fan or two CFLs and a fan for five to six hours came in. The trigger was to expand the market. There is a vast body of small shop owners and traders who need devices like inverters but cannot afford them. Su-Kam came up with the idea of a small portable device. The trader can carry it with him when he goes to his shop during the day, use it for uninterrupted power, and when he returns home at night can carry it back with him, again getting a night of uninterrupted power. The entire package, including battery, weighs about seven kg. The inverter costs only Rs 2000 (Rs 4000 with battery). Su-Kam has also tied up finance offers with this.

The Two Patented Softwares

Su-Kam doesn't just produce hardware. It also produces the software to run it.

The first software created was the PowerDoc Monitoring system, which helps in remote monitoring all the larger KVA products sold by Su-Kam. On a single graph, one can see the performance of the grid power and inverter power anywhere in the world.

The second breakthrough innovation is the Recall Software through which a Su-Kam servicing or maintenance man can find out, without having to open the inverter, how a particular inverter has been used over the last two or three days. It also points out the potential areas of fault and immediate possible remedies. This helps in rapid diagnosis and online correction of faults.

A Culture of Innovation

Running an innovative organization isn't possible without creating an innovation culture. Kunwer doesn't just employ people he thinks would fit in best with the job requirement. He also manages to inspire and push for constant research and development in his company. What is his approach towards cultivating an innovative work environment in the organization? His strategy for this is two-pronged:

What is Su-Kam the organization like? The impression one gets after a visit to Su-Kam and speaking to the team is 'world-beaters'. The standards, the constant innovations, the attention to detail in a thousand little things from appraisals to recruitment to dealer meets, to product innovations and manufacturing innovations and the sheer pride that people at Su-Kam display in the work they are doing are frankly breathtaking. If you want to learn what it takes to create a world-beater that transforms an industry, make a pilgrimage to Su-Kam. If you want to learn how to create an environment of constant innovation, and sheer ongoing and continuous challenging of the status quo, go to Su-Kam.

1.   He believes that to motivate an employee effectively, 'his confidence in you should be very high. If you are not able to create that, why should he work for you? He has to see his future unfolding in your organization.' Su-Kam is very clearly a meritocracy. People grow in proportion to their output.

2.   He ensures that every employee has the liberty to experiment. He says, 'I'm a person of experiments, and I allow people to experiment.' And he certainly walks the talk. An example of this comes from the time when the company was only manufacturing inverters up to 40 KVA. The R&D team decided to try making a 100-KVA inverter, the first of its kind in India. Imagine the challenge: instead of growing incrementally from 40 to 50 to 60 KVA, they wanted to go directly from 40 to 100 KVA. When the figures were worked out, the cost of project turned out to be around Rs 25 lakhs! A big sum for what was then a small company. When Kunwer was approached, he said, 'Yes!' And today Su-Kam is the only company in India and the second in the world that can boast of a 100-KVA

What if empowerment were not the freedom to take decisions but the freedom to make mistakes? What kind of culture would we then have in organizations? The two are not necessarily the same. I can give you the freedom to take decisions and then jump on you, hold you rigidly accountable and take you to task for any mistakes. On the other hand, I can give you the freedom to make mistakes and hold you accountable to correct them so that we both develop and grow along the way. What if more organizations were designed like the latter?

inverter! As Sanjeev in R&D puts it, 'Things may fail initially, but eventually we *will* make it work. One may not succeed the first time, but when someone gives you the space to think, the liberty to do things which are sometimes beyond your limits, you can innovate.'

Moving forward, Kunwer plans to make every home a source of power generation. His team is working on a grid interacting inverter, in which a person would be both drawing from and uploading power to the grid. Su-Kam envisions moving to solar energy and making each home a net power generator. With the whole world moving towards collaborative networks and individuals generating value to communities over the Internet, why should power be any different? It is an industrial age concept that power has to be centrally generated and distributed. In the next few years, every home should be able to generate its own power and the grid only used to balance power requirements across geographies.

AFTERWORD

George Bernard Shaw had it right when he said that all progress depends on the unreasonable man. Orbit shifting, however, isn't about being unreasonable for the sake of being unreasonable. Nor is it about challenging things for the sake of challenging them. Without a clear purpose, nothing will work. The purpose is the compass. And the purpose comes from the orbit-shifting challenge—something that is both unreasonable *and* unambiguous. Think 'eliminate unnecessary blindness' or 'eliminate Hepatitis B' or 'leaders from Day One'. You can't get more unreasonable and unambiguous than that.

An unreasonable challenge always needs one to break out of the boundaries of the industry's thinking. It needs enrolment of people who are inspired by the challenge, and it needs an almost fanatical eye on dilution. Every single day, inertia can seep in and dilution can take place so that the unreasonable challenge suddenly becomes so diluted and so reasonable that it doesn't shift any orbits at all.

Each of the orbit shifters we have discussed in this book has followed the principles of orbit shifting at the time of bringing alive their respective missions. Actually each of the missions is still alive and thriving. As often happens, over time, some may continue and grow in strength and some may fall by the wayside and let go of the principles that made them true orbit shifters. However, post-mission success or failure cannot take away from the orbit shifters what they created at that moment in time and in those particular circumstances. They changed the world as it existed!

A NOTE ON EREHWON INNOVATION CONSULTING AND MARICO INNOVATION FOUNDATION

Erehwon Innovation Consulting has brought to the world a pioneering approach and methodology: Orbit-shifting Innovation™. Erehwon has over sixteen years of hands-on experience of being able to instil innovation and shift orbits in the most legacy-driven and unresponsive environments across the industry spectrum. Organizations, globally, have recognized Erehwon's unique approach to innovation. The outcome of engaging with this breakthrough approach is usually a new orbit, which infuses new aspirations, new energy and new directions to achieve quantum innovation by design. To learn more, please visit www.erehwonconsulting.com.

Marico Innovation Foundation, promoted by Marico, an Indian FMCG major, was created in March 2003 under the stewardship of Dr Ramesh Mashelkar (former director general, CSIR, and currently president, Global Research Alliance), with a single mission: to fuel innovation in India. The Foundation believes that the only way to bring alive its mission of disseminating innovation in India is to first learn. It has, therefore, along with Erehwon Innovation Consulting, undertaken research into areas concerning India and innovation, through the 'Breakthrough in India' series, to get to the heart of the matter and to understand how it really happens. The result of the research is the book you hold in your hands. The Foundation intends to propagate these findings through large-scale mass platforms across India. The Foundation also organizes the prestigious annual Innovation for India Awards that highlight innovations in the business sector, the social sector and in the business for social sector.

Some of the most eminent and influential innovation leaders in the country came together to form its governing council. The members are: Dr Ramesh Mashelkar; Anu Aga, chairperson, Thermax; Sam Balsara, CEO, Madison; Ashwin Dani, vice chairman, Asian Paints; Ranjan Kapur, country manager, WPP; Arun Maira, chairman, Boston Consulting Group, India; Harsh Mariwala, chairman, Marico Industries Ltd; K.V. Mariwala, former director, Marico Ltd; Rajiv Narang, chairman and MD, Erehwon Innovation Consulting; and Dorab Sopariwala, consultant. To learn more, please visit www.maricoinnovationfoundation.org.